ENCYCLOPEDIA OF
SPACE

ENCYCLOPEDIA OF
SPACE

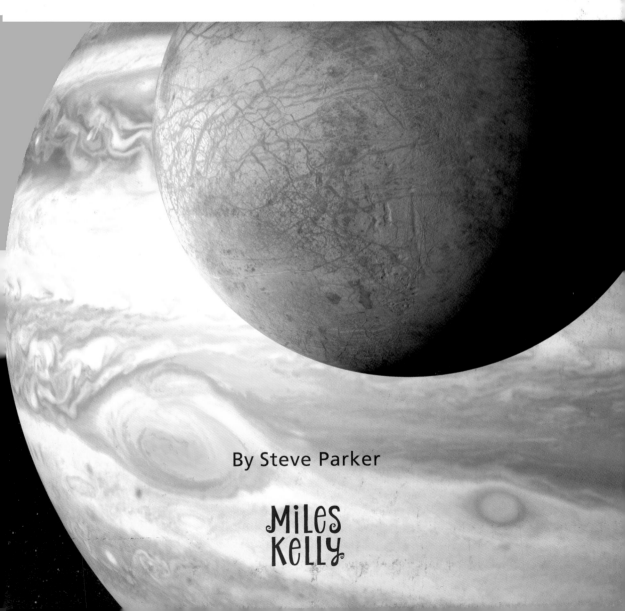

By Steve Parker

Miles Kelly

First published in 2017 by Miles Kelly Publishing Ltd
Harding's Barn, Bardfield End Green, Thaxted, Essex, CM6 3PX, UK

Copyright © Miles Kelly Publishing Ltd 2017

This edition printed 2018

4 6 8 10 9 7 5 3

Publishing Director Belinda Gallagher
Creative Director Jo Cowan
Editorial Director Rosie Neave
Senior Editor Claire Philip
Design Manager Simon Lee
Image Manager Liberty Newton
Indexer Marie Lorimer
Production Elizabeth Collins, Caroline Kelly
Reprographics Stephan Davis, Jennifer Cozens, Thom Allaway
Assets Lorraine King
Contributors Steve Parker, Sue Becklake, John Farndon,
Tim Furniss, Clint Twist

ISBN 978-1-78617-329-4

Printed in China

British Library Cataloguing-in-Publication Data
A catalogue record for this book is available from the British Library

Made with paper from a sustainable forest

www.mileskelly.net

Contents

The Universe

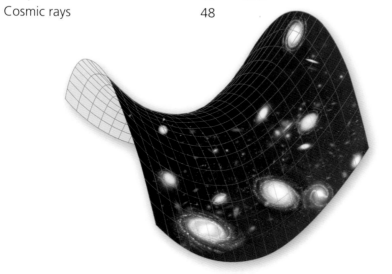

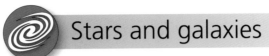

Stars and galaxies

The Solar System

Astronomy

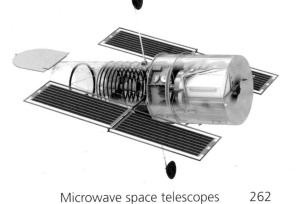

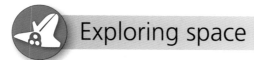

Exploring space

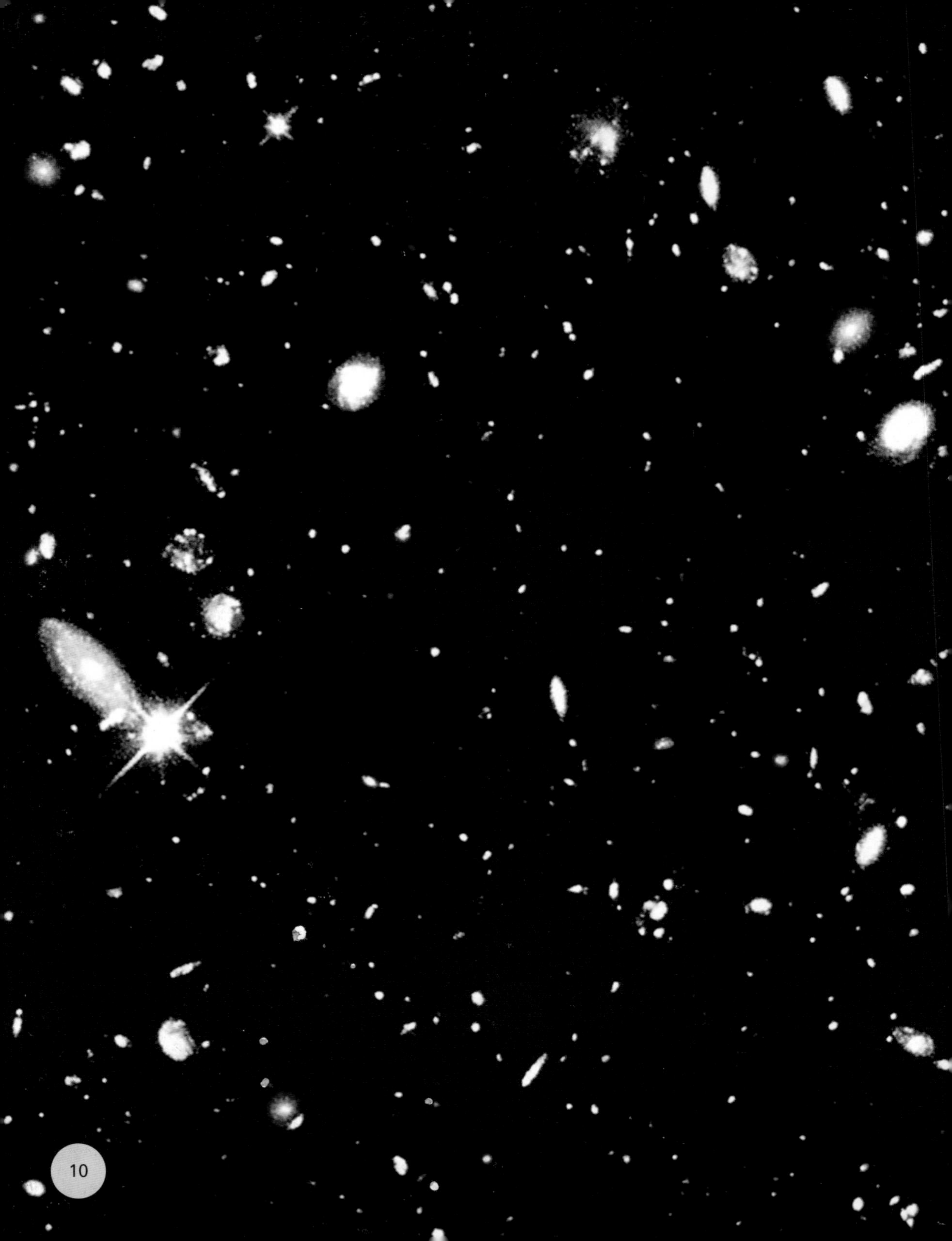

The Universe

What is space?

🪐 **Space is the word used to describe** everywhere that is not Earth and its surrounding layer of air, the atmosphere.

🪐 **The generally accepted point** where the atmosphere fades to almost nothing, and space begins, is 100 km above Earth's surface.

🪐 **The region around our Solar System** is known as local space, while the space between the stars in our galaxy, the Milky Way, is known as interstellar space. Beyond that is intergalactic space.

🪐 **Space is not an empty vacuum** – it is a near vacuum, called the interstellar medium. Each cubic kilometre contains a few drifting atoms of gas and dust, as well as many forms of energy.

🪐 **In the region of the Sun**, this interstellar medium consists of about 90 percent hydrogen, 9 percent helium and one percent dust.

🪐 **The interstellar dust** consists of tiny grains composed mainly of silicate (silicon and oxygen) and graphite (carbon), as well as small amounts of iron.

🪐 **Between galaxies**, the intergalactic medium consists mostly of ionized hydrogen – atoms of hydrogen gas each with its single electron stripped away, so it consists of just one proton.

🪐 **Space is so enormous** that common units of measurement such as miles and kilometres become meaningless – which is why people often use the word 'astronomical' to describe exceptionally large numbers.

🪐 **In local space**, distances are often measured in AUs (Astronomical Units). One AU is the average distance between the Earth and the Sun – about 150 million km (specifically 149,597,871 km).

Interstellar space distances are usually measured in light years (ly). One light year is the distance light travels in one year – about 9.5 trillion km (specifically 9,460,730,472,580.8 km).

Some astronomers prefer to measure large distances in parsecs (pc). One parsec equals 3.26 light years. A kiloparsec (kpc) is 1000 parsecs and a megaparsec (mpc) is 1,000,000 parsecs.

▼ *The Andromeda Galaxy (M31), the nearest spiral galaxy to our own, is here viewed across 780 kiloparsecs (about 2.5 million light years) of intergalactic space.*

The Universe

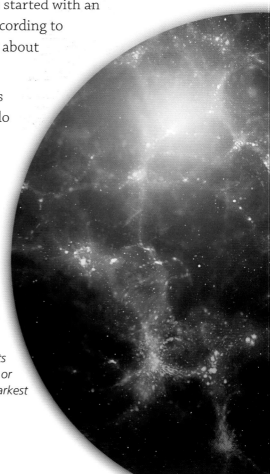

The Universe is everything that we can ever know – all of space and all of time. Before the Universe came into existence there was nothingness, no space, no time, no energy and no matter.

The study of the Universe – its history, future, and large-scale features – is known as cosmology.

Scientists believe that the Universe started with an explosion known as the Big Bang. According to latest estimates, the Universe is now about 13.8 billion years old.

Since the Big Bang the Universe has been expanding and it continues to do so. The most distant galaxies are moving away from us at about 90 percent of the speed of light.

The Universe was once thought to be everything that could ever exist, but recent theories suggest that our Universe may be just one of countless bubbles of space-time.

▶ This computer image shows the general structure of the Universe. The larger light spots are superclusters of galaxies, linked by strings or filaments of smaller groups of galaxies. The darkest areas are vast tracts of thin gases and dust.

▶ *The Universe is getting bigger all the time as galaxies rush outwards in all directions.*

🌀 **Although there is no maximum** possible temperature in the Universe, there is a very precise minimum possible temperature. The third law of thermodynamics states that it is impossible for anything to be cooled to absolute zero (−273°C).

🌀 **Working in specialized laboratories**, scientists have cooled substances to within a billionth of a degree of absolute zero, but they cannot achieve this ultimate low temperature.

🌀 **Matter is not distributed** evenly throughout the Universe. On the largest scale, the Universe consists of thin filaments, each one made up of millions of galaxies, which surround vast voids that contain nothing but clouds of intergalactic hydrogen.

🌀 **The largest structure** yet identified is an extended line of galaxies known as the Great Wall that is located about 500 million light years from our galaxy.

The size and shape of the Universe

🪐 **Over the centuries** there have been many proposals for the size and shape of the Universe.

🪐 **Ancient cultures** had many theories about the Universe. They often believed that the Earth was at its centre.

🪐 **These historical ideas** included the belief that the Universe was a ball in the hand of a giant human.

🪐 **Another myth** was that the Universe emerged from a giant egg, laid by a black-winged bird.

🪐 **One modern suggestion** is that the Universe has no measurable size and shape, that is, it is infinite and goes on for ever in all directions.

🪐 **Other proposals** for its shape include an irregular blob, a vast sphere or ball, a flattish slab with rounded corners, and a giant doughnut-like torus.

▶ *These images show three likely possible shapes for the Universe. One is the Flat Universe (1) – although it looks thin, its top-bottom distance is many billions of kilometres. The ball shape (2) is known as the Closed Universe. The saddle-like shape (3) with two sets of curves is called the Open Universe.*

1

- **The Universe has four dimensions,** called space-time – three of normal space (up/down, left/right, forward/backward), plus time. Calculations involving space-time give three possible Universe shapes.

- **These shapes are:** flat like a sheet of paper (planar), closed like a ball (spherical) and open curves like the saddle of a horse (hyperbolic).

- **The observable Universe** is what we can detect and estimate from our observations and measurements.

- **Using these estimates** the Universe seems to be about 90 billion light years across, which is 855 billion trillion km.

> **DID YOU KNOW?**
> Whatever its size and shape, it is known that the Universe is expanding, and that its speed of expansion is increasing.

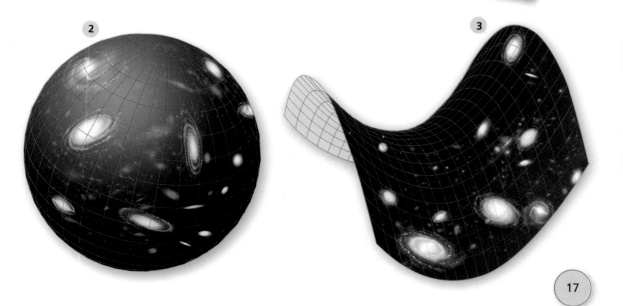

2

3

The Multiverse proposal

People have long wondered whether the Universe is part of something bigger, such as a multiverse – many universes, maybe side by side, one inside another, or even separate.

▼ *Multiple flat universes may be stacked next to each other, as shown here. Another possibility is that each one may be inside the next, larger one. Or there may be one main universe with smaller ones embedded (set into) it.*

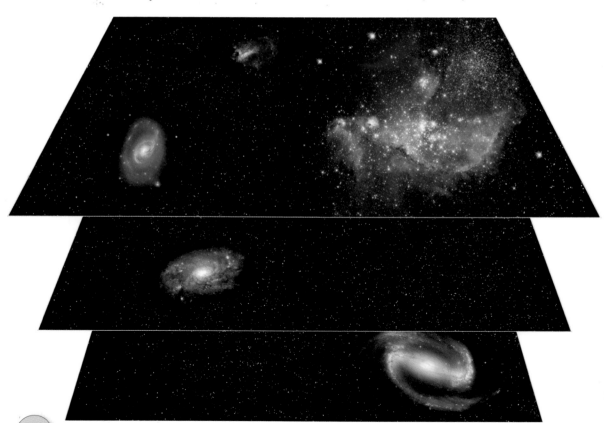

Other proposals include parallel universes, alternate universes, and those involving extra dimensions and additional realities.

Some of these ideas are based on three-dimensional shapes that exist in daily life.

One approach is to think of the Universe we observe as being surrounded by another universe on an even greater scale, and so on, becoming more enormous each time, like a series of spheres inside each other.

Another proposal is to view 'our' Universe as one bubble which is part of a multi-bubble system, with some bubbles shrinking or merging, while others expand or divide into more bubbles.

Some ideas involve the Hubble bubble (Hubble sphere or volume). This is a huge ball-shaped or spherical region. On its outside, space and its objects are racing away faster than the speed of light. So any light travelling towards the centre of the bubble never gets there.

Some multiverses are described in terms of mathematics and have more dimensions than the usual three we can picture.

Mathematical multiverses may have 7, 10, 11 or more dimensions.

A further set of theories involve time progressing at different rates in different universes. This would mean that even if two universes start out much the same, they will evolve at varying rates and soon become different.

The Big Bang

🪐 **Events happened very quickly** at the beginning of the Universe. In order to explain what happened scientists use measurements of time that are as small as one ten million trillion trillion trillionth of a second.

🪐 **At first the Universe** was indescribably small and hot. It has been getting larger and cooler ever since.

🪐 **In its initial state**, the four fundamental forces (strong and weak nuclear forces, electromagnetism and gravity) were unified into a single force.

🪐 **Gravity was the first of the four forces** to separate, followed by the strong nuclear force. This triggered an event known as inflation and the Universe suddenly became billions of billions times bigger.

🪐 **About one-billionth of a second** after the Big Bang, the Universe consisted of a dense sea of quarks and other particles.

🪐 **About three minutes** after the Big Bang there was a brief period of nucleosynthesis when quarks joined together to form neutrons and protons.

🪐 **For the first 300,000 years** the Universe remained completely opaque. Then it became cool enough for protons and neutrons to capture electrons and form atoms. The Universe was now transparent.

🪐 **About 100 million years** after the Big Bang, the first stars began to shine.

🪐 **There is still** much to be discovered about the Universe and the Big Bang.

▲ *No one knows what the Big Bang looked like 13.8 million years ago, so it is usually shown as some kind of explosion. However at its very beginning, forces and matter were very different. Not even light as we know it existed.*

Scientists have recently proposed that there must be a fifth fundamental force (known as dark energy or quintessence) that prevents the Universe from collapsing inwards under the force of its own gravity.

Inflation phase

🪐 **Cosmic or cosmological inflation** is the very short amount of time immediately after the Big Bang, which happened around 13.8 billion years ago.

🪐 **The traditional explanation** tells how the Big Bang happened to a tiny point, which contained all the Universe's matter and energy. This is called the initial singularity.

🪐 **The inflationary phase**, when the Universe grew at its fastest rate, is measured in trillion-trillion-trillionths of a second immediately after the Big Bang.

🪐 **During this extremely short period**, space may have expanded to half the size we see now in the observable Universe.

🪐 **This expansion** happened incredibly fast – at a speed which was faster than light. After inflation, this speed was no longer possible.

▶ *The inflation phase, when the Universe suddenly expanded greatly, happened almost immediately after the Big Bang – in less than a fraction of a fraction of a second.*

1 Big Bang

2 Inflation

3 Expansion occurs more smoothly

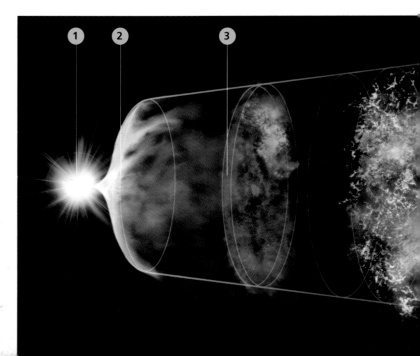

● **The fundamental forces** of nature also came into being, with gravity emerging – possibly as gravitational waves.

● **There may have been** early irregularities and inconsistencies in the ways that space, energy, forces and time spread out. But if they did exist these fluctuations flattened out so that space then spread out more evenly and smoothly.

● **Temperatures also dropped** during the inflationary phase, from immeasurably hot, perhaps 1000 trillion trillion trillion°C, to 10,000 trillion trillion°C.

● **Newer explanations** about what happened after the Big Bang try to take quantum theory into account, which applies at the tiniest scales of atoms and the particles that make them.

Dark Ages

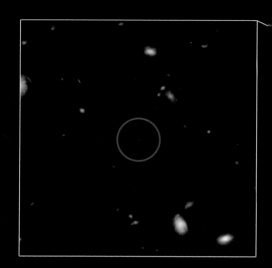

➤ *This image, taken by the Hubble Space Telescope shows galaxy UDFy-38135539 near the farthest visible part of the Universe, 13.1 billion light years away. It formed during the Universe's reionization phase.*

The Dark Ages of the Universe probably began 100–150 million years after the Big Bang. By this time, various forms of matter had come into existence.

This matter consisted of the particles inside atoms, such as protons and electrons. They has previously existed together, as whole atoms. But as the Universe's heat energy grew, the particles separated and became free, known as ions.

The Dark Ages began when energy cooled again and the particles began to come back together as atoms. They formed mainly the simplest atoms – those of hydrogen.

These hydrogen atoms were not charged, but neutral.

There was so much neutral hydrogen that it blocked the spread of the limited amount of light at the time.

As time passed, and energy and temperature levels changed, some atoms began to separate again, forming charged particles known as ionized plasma, a period known as reionization.

Also during this time, the first stars began to form and shine

 **Gradually the Dark Ages faded**, probably between 500 and 1000 million (0.5 and 1 billion) years ago.

 **Evidence for the Dark Ages** and early star formation comes from the farthest objects we can see. For example, Galaxy MACS0647-JD is 13.3 billion light years away – so we are seeing it less than 500 million years after the Big Bang.

25

Star formation

🪐 **The stages in star formation** have been worked out by cosmologists and other scientists. They continue to study the stars that are still throughout space.

🪐 **Clouds of hydrogen**, other gases and space dust gradually clump together under their own gravity, drawing in more matter and becoming denser.

🪐 **Eventually the matter** becomes so hot and dense that the centres, or nuclei, of atoms begin to join or fuse.

🪐 **This nuclear fusion** gives off light, heat and other rays and energy – the star shines.

🪐 **This process** probably first started to happen around 200 million years after the Big Bang. Before this, it was too hot and energetic for atoms to undergo nuclear fusion.

🪐 **The Sloan Digital Sky Survey** (SDSS) is a project to map and measure the distances of millions of galaxies, stars and other objects from Earth.

🪐 **The survey** is specialized to detect the feature called red shift. Combined with other evidence, this indicates the distance of a star or galaxy from Earth, and the direction and speed at which it is moving.

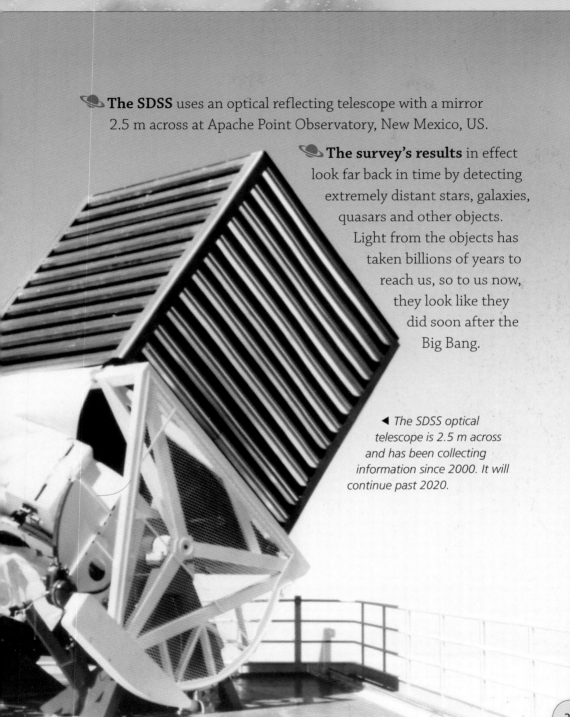

The SDSS uses an optical reflecting telescope with a mirror 2.5 m across at Apache Point Observatory, New Mexico, US.

The survey's results in effect look far back in time by detecting extremely distant stars, galaxies, quasars and other objects. Light from the objects has taken billions of years to reach us, so to us now, they look like they did soon after the Big Bang.

◄ *The SDSS optical telescope is 2.5 m across and has been collecting information since 2000. It will continue past 2020.*

The rise of dark matter

🪐 **In the 20th century**, as cosmologists and astrophysicists learned more about the Universe, questions began to arise.

🪐 **The overall structure**, gravity, size, expansion rate, amount of energy and other features of the Universe could not be simply explained using 'ordinary' matter of atoms and molecules.

🪐 **The idea of dark matter** arose as an explanation. The theory that there must be something mysterious and unseen was first developed in the 1930s, by astronomers such as Jan Oort (1990–1992).

🪐 **In the 1960s–1970s** suspicions grew further that in addition to ordinary matter and energy, there must be something else.

🪐 **Dark matter** and its counterpart dark energy are so named because they are mysterious and so far undetected.

🪐 **Today, dark matter** and dark energy are assumed to exist by scientists – but in the timeline of the Universe, when did dark matter itself arise?

🪐 **One proposal** is the Lambda Cold Dark Matter (LCDM) model. This suggests that dark matter is made of extremely cold, slow, tiny particles that give out no light or other electromagnetic waves, which is why they are so difficult to find. These dark matter particles could have perhaps come into existence several thousand years after the Big Bang.

🪐 **Other calculations** put the appearance of dark matter at tens of millions of years after the Big Bang.

▶ *The galaxy cluster Abell 1689 contains more than 1000 galaxies, which suggests it also has immense amounts of dark matter, the gravity of which is affecting its expansion.*

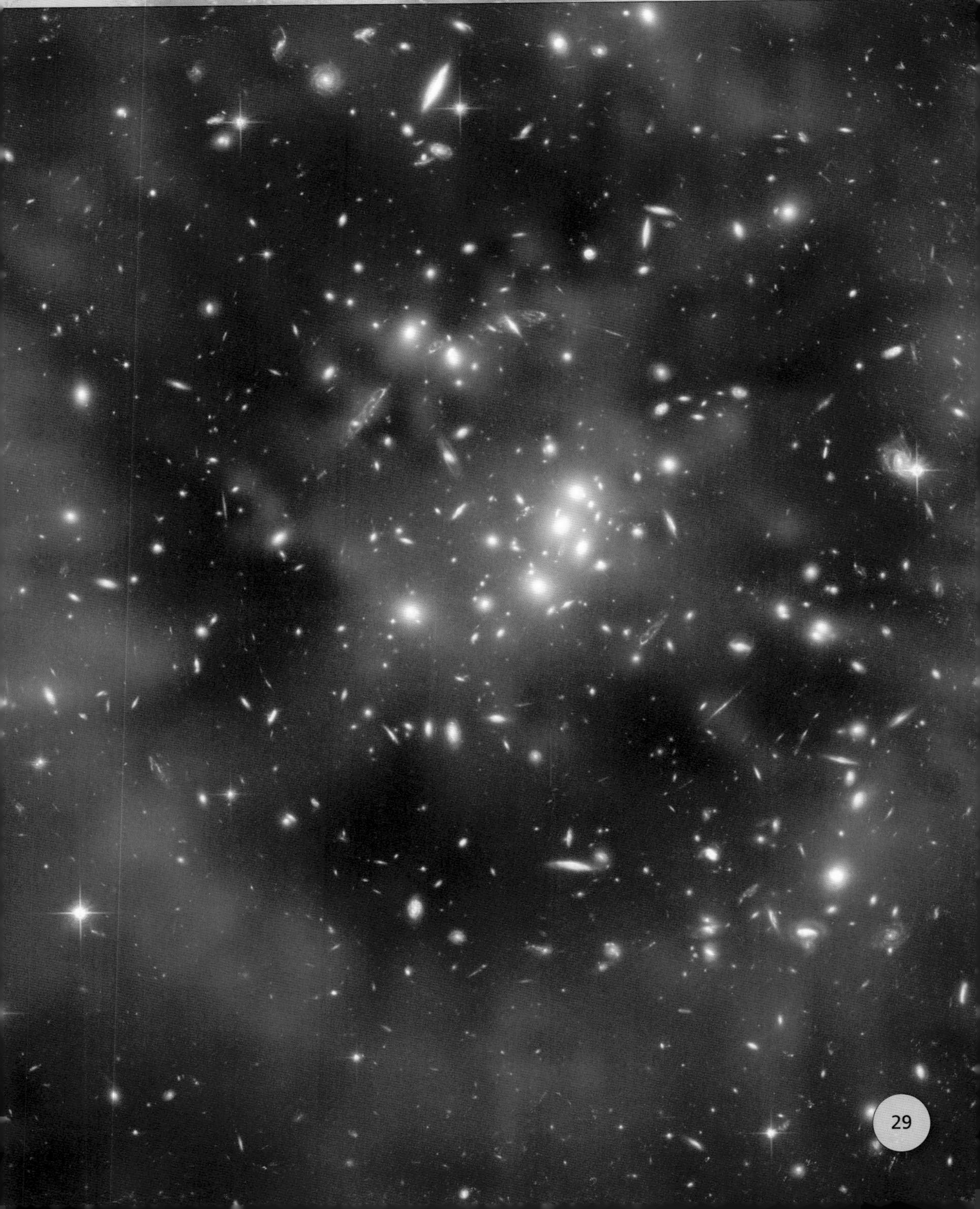

Microwave background

🪐 **The faint 'echoes' of the Big Bang** have been detected in the form of a cosmic microwave background radiation that pervades the whole Universe.

🪐 **Background radiation** shows that the temperature of the Big Bang has now cooled to about 2.7°C above Absolute Zero.

🪐 **American radio engineers** Arno Penzias (1933–) and Robert Wilson (1936–) discovered the microwave background in 1965, while trying to find the source of radio 'noise' that was interfering with communications.

🪐 **At one time** they thought that pigeon droppings on their antennae might be causing the interference, but after a thorough cleaning the noise remained.

🪐 **Eventually, they determined** that the source of the noise was located beyond the Milky Way galaxy, and that the signal appeared to be coming from all directions.

🪐 **US physicist George Gamow** (1904–1968) predicted the existence of microwave background radiation in 1947, although he believed it would be slightly warmer at around 10°C above Absolute Zero.

🪐 **In 1993, the first images** of this radiation were produced by the Cosmic Background Explorer (COBE) spacecraft.

🪐 **The COBE images** showed that the radiation was uniform to within one part in a thousand throughout the Universe, with minute ripples showing areas that were fractionally warmer or cooler.

🪐 **A subsequent survey** by instruments aboard the WMAP satellite has provided a more accurate picture that shows how the distribution of temperature fluctuations in the background radiation exactly mirrors the large-scale structure of the Universe.

🪐 **Slightly cooler regions were denser** and contained the matter that eventually condensed into the filaments of galaxies, while the slightly warmer regions became empty voids.

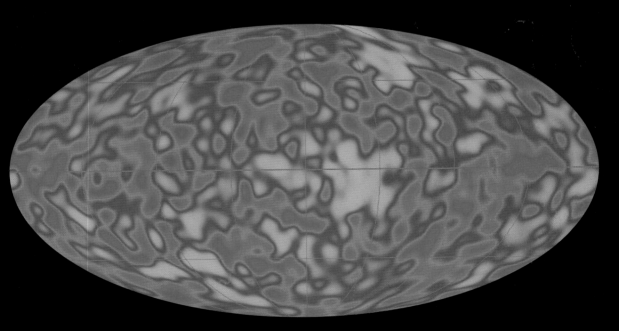

▲ *This famous image of the Universe's microwave background was obtained from information collected by the COBE satellite. Pink areas are slightly warmer and blues are cooler, but these temperature differences are extremely tiny.*

Objects

🪐 **The Universe consists of energy and matter** irregularly distributed throughout the continuum of space-time, but most of the matter and energy is invisible to humans.

🪐 **Scientists now believe** that the Universe is made up of 68 percent dark energy, 27 percent dark matter, and about 5 percent ordinary 'luminous' matter we can detect, in the form of stars and galaxies.

▼ *This bright galaxy is a single astronomical object, even though it contains billions of individual stars and is constantly forming new clusters of stars.*

- **The ordinary 'luminous' matter** is clumped together in objects of varying sizes and densities. The term 'object' refers to individual items that astronomers can examine through telescopes.

- **On Earth**, matter exists naturally mainly in three forms: gas, liquid and solid. There is a fourth form of matter – a completely ionized gas known as plasma – that can be made in the laboratory and occurs rarely in nature, as in lightning.

- **Beyond Earth's atmosphere**, however, plasma (where atoms lose their electrons) is extremely common and is the main component of the 'wind' produced by stars and the intergalactic medium.

- **The largest commonly** named astronomical objects are galaxies, followed in terms of diminishing size by nebulae, stars, planets, moons, asteroids, comets and meteorites.

- **Although galaxies are made** of many billions of stars, they are considered to be single objects. This is because their stars orbit around a common centre of gravity and have the same relative motion with respect to the rest of the Universe.

- **Astronomical objects** tend towards a spherical shape because a sphere has balanced gravitational forces all over its surface.

- **Objects of less than 200–400 km** in diameter, depending on what they are made of, have insufficient mass to achieve a spherical shape, which is why the smaller asteroids all have irregular shapes. This size is known as the 'potato limit'.

Laws of nature

🪐 **Scientists can learn more about the Universe** by discovering the natural laws that govern the behaviour of matter and energy and the relationships between them.

🪐 **William of Occam** (*c.*1287–1347), an English philosopher, established the guiding principle behind natural laws. Known as 'Occam's Razor', this principle states that 'hypotheses should not be multiplied without reason', meaning that the simplest explanation is likely to be correct.

🪐 **In addition to his law of universal gravitation**, Isaac Newton (1642–1727) also established three laws of motion that govern the movement of all objects larger than an atom, unless they are moving at close to the speed of light.

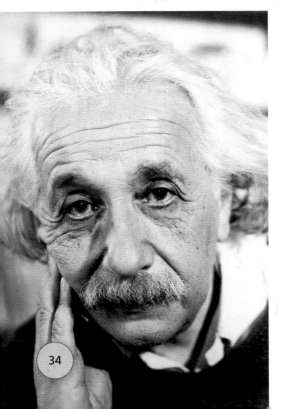

🪐 **Albert Einstein** (1879–1955) developed a theory of relativity that extended Newton's laws to include objects that are moving at near-light speed.

🪐 **Einstein's theory of relativity** led to his discovery that matter can be transformed into energy according to the famous equation $e=mc^2$, where 'e' is energy, 'm' is mass and 'c' is the speed of light.

◀ *Albert Einstein discovered some of the mathematical laws that govern the relationship between time and space, and energy and matter.*

Four mathematical equations devised by the Scottish physicist James Clerk Maxwell (1831–1879) describe phenomena associated with electricity and magnetism, and were used to predict the existence of the electromagnetic spectrum.

In 1931, the Indian astronomer Subramanyan Chandrasekhar (1910–1995) proved that no white dwarf star could have a mass of more than 1.4 times the mass of the Sun. Any stars that exceed this mass will explode as supernovae rather than shrink to become white dwarfs.

According to Hubble's law, first stated by Edwin Hubble (1889–1953) in 1929, the speed at which a galaxy appears to be moving away from us is proportional to its distance. The most distant galaxies are moving the fastest.

▶ *English scientist Isaac Newton published his three laws of motion in the 1680s. They apply well to everyday situations but Albert Einstein's laws from the 1900s–1910s are more accurate for astronomical distances, speeds and matter.*

LAWS OF MOTION	
Law 1	An object does not move unless something forces it to (inertia). It will go on moving at the same speed and in the same direction unless forced to change (momentum).
Law 2	The greater the mass of an object, the more force is needed to make it speed up, slow down, or change direction.
Law 3	For every action, there is an equal opposite reaction – in other words, when something pushes off in one direction, the thing it's pushing from is pushed back with equal force in the opposite direction.

Distances

- **The distance to the planets** is measured by bouncing radar signals off them and timing how long the signals take to get there and back.

- **The distance of nearby stars** is calculated by measuring the slight shift in the angle of each star in comparison to faraway stars, as the Earth orbits the Sun. This is called parallax shift.

- **Parallax shift can only be used** to measure nearby stars, so astronomers work out the distance to faraway stars and galaxies by comparing how bright they look with how bright they actually are.

- **For middle distance stars**, astronomers compare colour with brightness using the Hertzsprung-Russell (H-R) diagram. This is called main sequence fitting.

- **Beyond 30,000 light years**, stars are too faint for main sequence fitting to work.

- **Distances to nearby galaxies** can be estimated using 'standard candles' – stars that astronomers know the brightness of, such as supergiants and supernovae.

- **The expected brightness** of a galaxy that is too far away to pick out its stars may be measured using the Tully-Fisher technique, based on how fast galaxies spin.

> **DID YOU KNOW?**
> A laser beam is used to measure the distance to the Moon.

🪐 **Counting planetary nebulae** (the rings of gas left behind by supernovae explosions) is another way of measuring how bright a distant galaxy should be.

🪐 **A third method** of calculating the brightness of a distant galaxy is to gauge how mottled it looks.

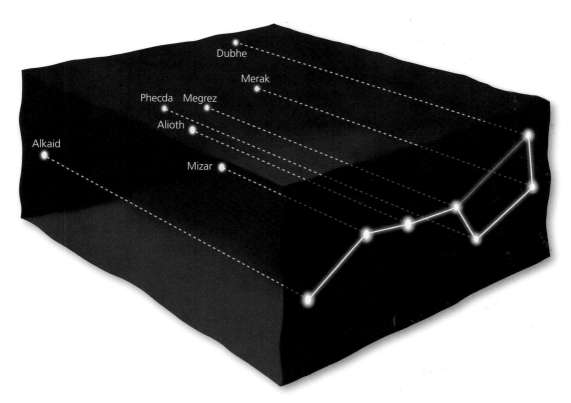

▲ *Seen from Earth, the stars in a constellation (such as this part of the Big Dipper) can appear to be all the same distance away. However, some may be much nearer than others.*

Light years

🪐 **Distances in space** are so vast that the fastest thing in the Universe, light, is used to measure them. The speed of light is about 300,000 km/sec.

🪐 **A light second is the distance** that light travels in one second – 300 million km.

🪐 **A light year is the distance** that light travels in one year – 9.46 trillion km.

🪐 **Light years** are one of the standard distance measurements in astronomy.

🪐 **It takes about eight minutes** for light from the Sun to reach Earth.

🪐 **Light takes 4.22 years** to reach Earth from the Sun's nearest star, Proxima Centauri. This means the star is 4.22 light years away – more than 40 trillion km.

🪐 **Viewed from Earth**, Proxima Centauri looks like it did 4.22 years ago because its light takes 4.22 years to reach Earth.

🪐 **The star Deneb** is 1800 light years away, which means it looks like it did when Emperor Septimus Severius ruled Rome (in AD 200).

🪐 **Astronomers use parsecs** to measure distances. They originally came from parallax shift measurements. A light year is 0.3066 parsecs.

DID YOU KNOW?
With powerful telescopes, astronomers can see galaxies over 13 billion light years away.

Sirius: 8.6 light years away

◄ *Three of the four telescopes that make up the Very Large Telescope in Chile, South America, gaze at the night sky. Brightest is Sirius, the 'Dog Star', about 8.6 light years distant.*

Light

🪐 **Light**, the fastest thing in the Universe, travels in straight lines.

🪐 **As they pass from one material** to another, light rays change direction. This is called refraction.

🪐 **Colours are different wavelengths** of light.

🪐 **The longest light waves** that can be seen are red, and the shortest are violet.

🪐 **Light is a form** of electromagnetic radiation.

DID YOU KNOW?
Photons of light travel in waves just 380–750 nanometres (millionths of a millimetre) in length.

▼ *Light can be viewed as small packets of energy called photons. When a photon hits an atom, energy is produced as light, X-rays or radio waves.*

1 Photon hits atom

2 Electron receives extra energy and jumps away

3 Electron falls back

4 Pulse of energy is released

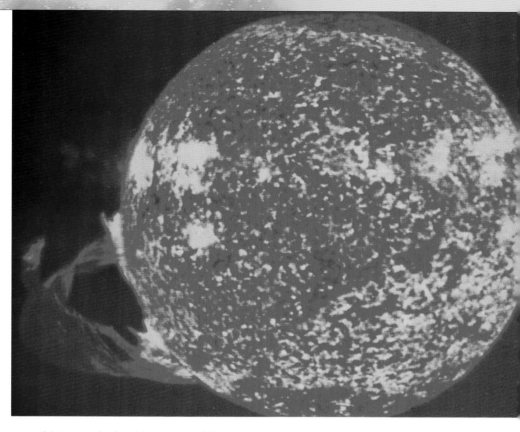

▲ *In this image the brightest areas of the Sun, giving out most light, are hottest. Here a huge solar flare leaps from the surface (lower left).*

🪐 **Faint light from very distant stars** is often recorded by sensors called CCDs. These count photons from the star as they arrive and build up a picture of the star over a long period.

🪐 **The electromagnetic spectrum** includes radio waves, ultraviolet light and X-rays. Visible light is the only part of the spectrum that can be seen by the human eye.

🪐 **Most light is given out by atoms**, and atoms give out light when 'excited', perhaps by radiation.

Red shift

- **When distant galaxies** are moving away from Earth, the light waves they give off are stretched out behind them. This is because each bit of the light wave is being sent from a little further away.

- **When the light waves** from distant galaxies are stretched out in this way, they look redder. This is called red shift.

- **Red shift was first described** by Austrian mathematician Christian Doppler (1803–1853) in 1842.

- **Edwin Hubble** (1889–1953) showed that a galaxy's red shift is proportional to its distance. The further away a galaxy is, the greater its red shift and the faster it must be zooming away from Earth. This is known as Hubble's Law.

- **The increase of red shift** with distance proved that the Universe is growing bigger.

- **Only nearby galaxies** show no red shift at all.

- **The most distant galaxies** have red shifts of up to seven.

- **Red shift can be caused** by the expansion of the Universe, gravity or the effect of relativity.

- **Black holes may create** large red shifts.

▶ *Massive red shifts reveal that the most distant objects in the Universe are flying away from Earth at astonishing speeds – often approaching the speed of light.*

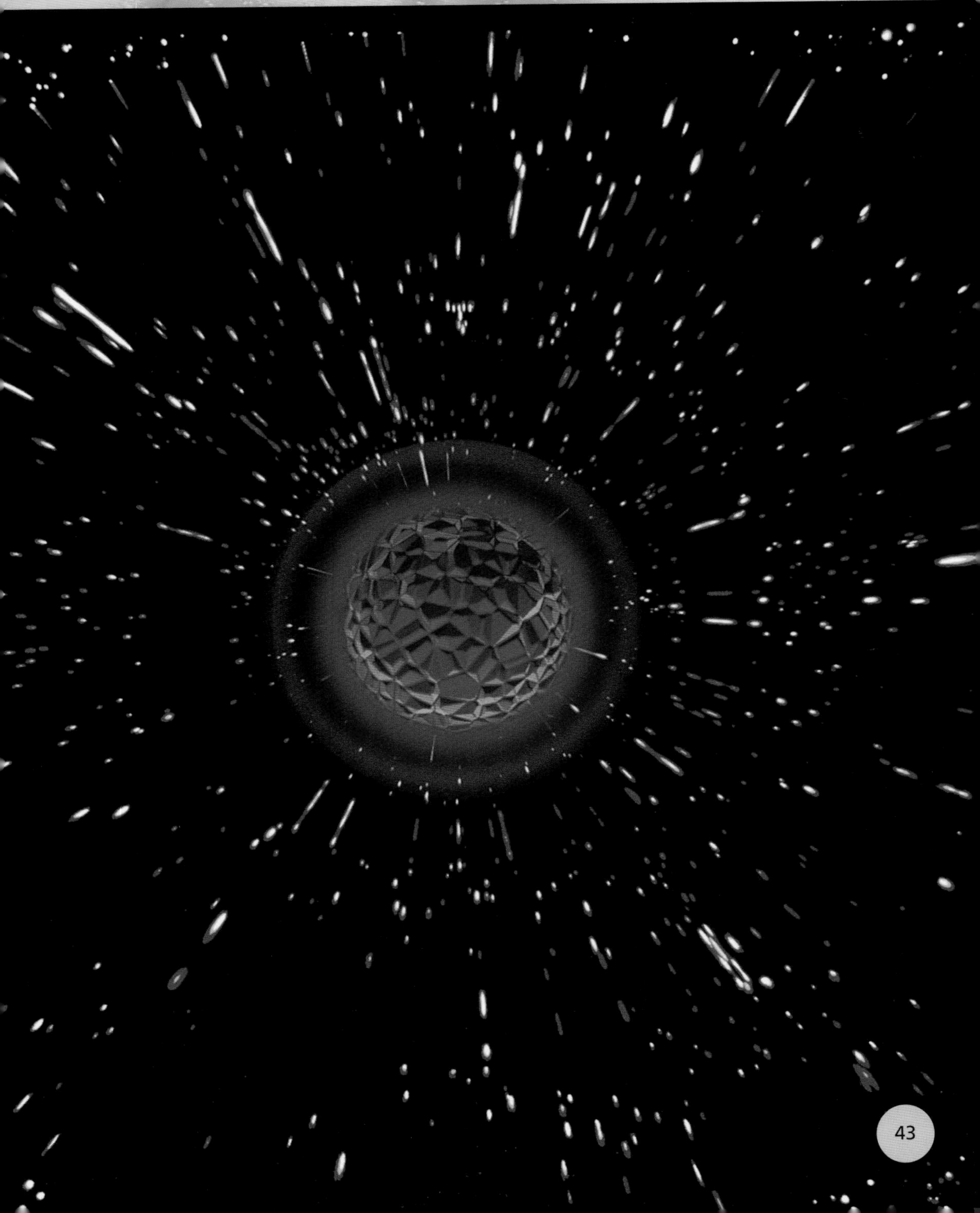

Radiation

🪐 **The energy that is given out** by atoms at high speed is called radiation. There are two main forms – atomic particles and electromagnetic radiation.

🪐 **Electromagnetic radiation either travels** as waves or as tiny particles called photons.

🪐 **Radioactivity is where an atom decays** (breaks down) and sends out gamma rays and particles.

🪐 **Nuclear radiation is generated** by atomic bombs and nuclear power stations.

🪐 **Electromagnetic radiation** is electric and magnetic fields that move photons in tiny bursts of waves.

🪐 **There are different kinds** of electromagnetic radiation, each with different wavelengths.

🪐 **Gamma rays** are a very short-wave, energetic and dangerous form of electromagnetic radiation.

🪐 **Radio waves** are a long wave, low-energy radiation.

▼ *Visible light is the only part of the electromagnetic spectrum that can be seen with the human eye.*

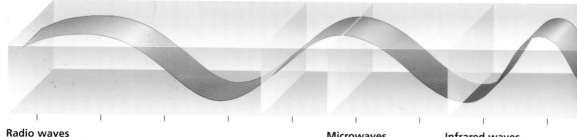

Radio waves   **Microwaves**   **Infrared waves**

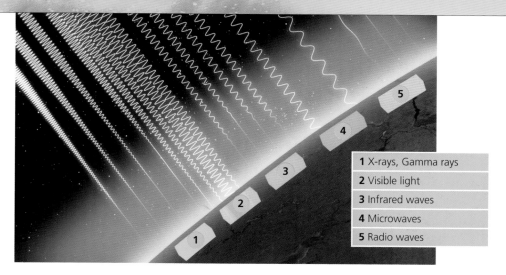

▲ *Earth's atmosphere absorbs or blocks some forms of electromagnetic radiation, such as the shortest X-ray and gamma waves. Light rays in particular make it through to the surface.*

1	X-rays, Gamma rays
2	Visible light
3	Infrared waves
4	Microwaves
5	Radio waves

🪐 **In between** gamma rays and radio waves are X-rays, ultraviolet rays, visible light, infrared rays and microwaves.

🪐 **Together, these forms** of electromagnetic radiation are called the electromagnetic spectrum.

🪐 **All electromagnetic rays** move at the speed of light – 299,792,458 m/sec.

🪐 **Objects in space** can be detected by the radiation that they give out, and perhaps by other features such as gravity.

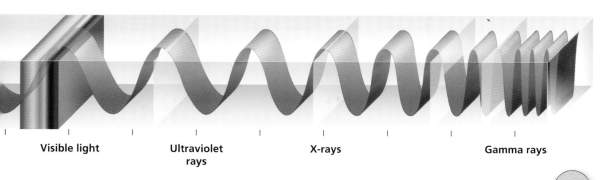

| Visible light | Ultraviolet rays | X-rays | Gamma rays |

X-rays

- **X-rays are electromagnetic rays** with waves shorter than ultraviolet rays and longer than gamma rays.

- **In space**, X-rays may be produced by very hot gases more than one million°C. They are also made when electrons interact with a magnetic field in synchrotron radiation (a kind of radiation).

- **X-rays cannot get through** Earth's atmosphere, so astronomers can only detect them using space telescopes, such as ROSAT, Chandra and XMM.

- **X-ray sources** are stars and galaxies that give out X-rays.

- **The first and brightest X-ray source** found (apart from the Sun) was the star Scorpius X-1 in 1962. Now tens of thousands are known, although most are weak.

- **Remnants of supernovae**, such as the Crab nebula, are strong sources of X-rays.

- **The strongest sources of X-rays** in the Milky Way are X-ray binaries such as Scorpius X-1 and Cygnus X-1. Some are thought to contain black holes.

- **X-ray binaries** pump out 1000 trillion times as much X-ray radiation as the Sun.

- **Outside the Milky Way**, X-ray galaxies harbouring big black holes are powerful X-ray sources.

▶ *This image of the Sun has two parts. One is a view of the Sun's extreme ultraviolet rays, invisible to our eyes but coloured by computer as orange. Overlaid on this are blue and green areas showing X-rays being given off by the Sun as detected by NASA's NuSTAR (Nuclear Spectroscopic Telescope Array), and again coloured by computer.*

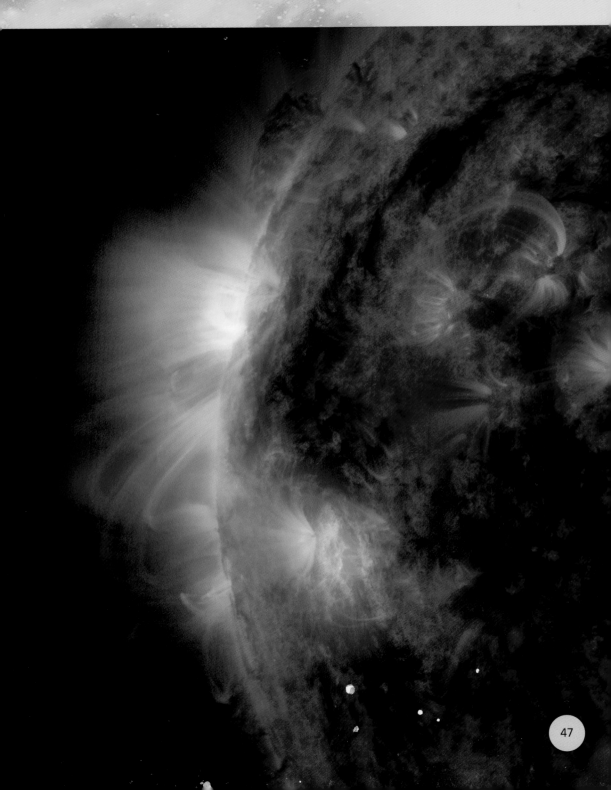

Cosmic rays

- **Streams of high-energy particles** that strike Earth's atmosphere are called cosmic rays.

- **The lowest-energy cosmic rays** come from the Sun, or are Galactic Cosmic Rays from outside the Solar System.

- **Medium-energy cosmic rays** come from sources within the Milky Way, including powerful supernovae explosions.

- **The highest-energy cosmic rays** may come from outside the Milky Way.

- **About 90 percent of GCRs** are the nuclei of hydrogen atoms stripped of their electron.

- **Most other GCRs** are helium and heavier nuclei, but there are also tiny positrons, electrons and neutrinos.

- **Neutrinos are so small** that they pass almost straight through the Earth without stopping.

- **The study of cosmic rays** provided scientists with most of their early knowledge about high-energy particles. On Earth, these particles can only be made in huge machines called particle accelerators.

- **Most cosmic rays** are deflected (pushed aside) by Earth's magnetic field or collide with particles in the atmosphere long before they reach the ground.

◄ *The Crab Nebula is the result of a supernova or exploding star. Its existence was first written about in 1054. In 1951 it was identified as a powerful source of cosmic rays.*

Gravity

🪐 **The attraction**, or pulling force, between all matter is gravity.

🪐 **Gravity holds everything on Earth** on the ground and stops it flying off into space. It holds Earth together, keeps the Moon in orbit around Earth, and Earth and other planets orbiting the Sun.

🪐 **Stars burn by squeezing** their matter together. This is caused by gravity.

🪐 **Gravity acts on all matter** in the Universe, probably in the form of gravitational waves, which were first discovered in 2016.

🪐 **The force of gravity** depends on mass (the amount of matter in an object) and distance.

🪐 **The more mass an object has**, and the closer it is to another object, the more strongly its gravity pulls.

🪐 **Black holes have the strongest** gravitational pull in the Universe.

🪐 **The basic laws of gravity** can be used for anything, including detecting an unseen planet by studying the flickers in another star's light.

▶ *Giant galaxies are so massive that their force of gravity may pull other, smaller galaxies towards them.*

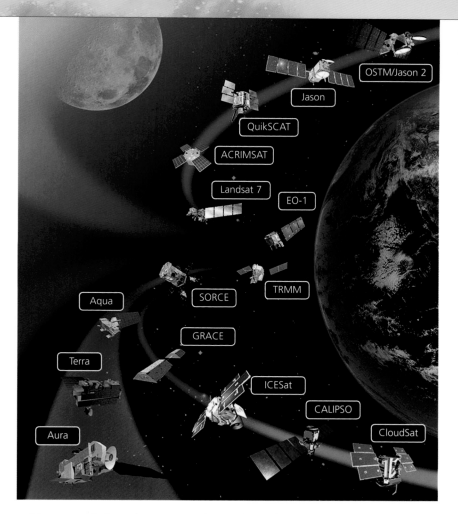

▲ *The correct balance between Earth's gravity and an object's mass and forward speed keeps hundreds of satellites in orbit around Earth.*

🪐 **Einstein's theory of general relativity** shows that gravity not only pulls on matter, but also bends space, and even time itself.

🪐 **Orbits are the result** of a perfect balance between the force of gravity on an object (which pulls it inward towards whatever it is orbiting) and its forward momentum (which keeps it flying straight onwards).

Mass and weight

🪐 **Mass and weight** are two terms that are often confused even though they are very different.

🪐 **The differences between them** may be unimportant in daily life, but they are central to space science and cosmology.

🪐 **Mass is the amount of matter** in an object, that is, the numbers and kinds of matter particles, such as atoms and molecules.

🪐 **The main unit** of mass is the kilogram.

🪐 **Mass gives an object** its gravity and associated features, such as how easily it is moved. Mass is not dependent on gravity and is the same anywhere in the Universe (except perhaps extreme places such as black holes).

🪐 **In contrast**, weight is dependent on gravity.

🪐 **An object's weight** is a measure of how hard gravity pulls on or attracts it, which in turn depends on where it is.

🪐 **Weight is a force**, measured in newtons. In daily life we measure weight in kilograms.

🪐 **Suppose an object** has a mass of 10 kg. On Earth's surface, pulled down by the planet's gravity, it would have a weight of 98 newtons.

🪐 **On the Moon**, which is smaller and has less gravity, the object's weight would be about 16 newtons.

🪐 **On Jupiter**, it would be nearer 230 newtons – but its mass would still be 10 kg.

▶ *Orbiting astronauts experience microgravity and are almost weightless. But their body mass is the same as on Earth.*

DID YOU KNOW?

One newton is the force of Earth's gravity acting on an average-sized apple – like the one that supposedly fell on Isaac Newton's head. This apple would 'weigh', that is, have a mass of, 102 g.

Dark matter

🪐 **Space matter that cannot be seen** is called dark matter. Unlike stars and galaxies, it does not give off light.

🪐 **There is much more dark matter** in the Universe than bright. Some scientists think 97 percent of all matter is dark.

▼ *This 3D map shows how dark matter has formed clumps in the Universe. Since dark matter cannot be detected directly, the map is produced from the effects of gravity and mass on light, and other information gathered by the Hubble Space Telescope. Normal visible matter that forms planets and stars is concentrated in the densest areas of dark matter.*

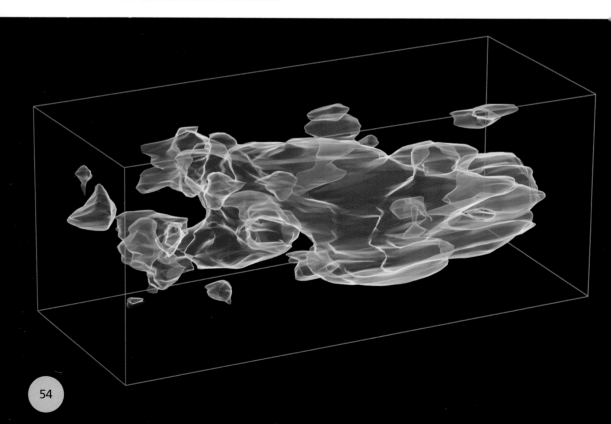

- **Astronomers know about dark matter** because its gravity pulls on stars and galaxies, changing their orbits and the way they rotate.

- **The visible stars in the Milky Way** galaxy are only a thin part, embedded in a big ball of dark matter.

- **Dark matter is of two kinds** – the matter in galaxies (galactic) and the matter between them (intergalactic).

- **Galactic dark matter** may be similar to ordinary matter. However, it burned out early in the life of the Universe.

- **Intergalactic dark matter** is made up of Weakly Interacting Massive Particles (WIMPs).

- **Some WIMPs** are called cold, dark matter, because they are travelling slowly.

- **Other WIMPs** are called hot, dark matter because they are travelling very quickly.

- **The future of the Universe** may depend on how much dark matter there is. If there is too much, its gravity will eventually stop the Universe's expansion, and make it shrink again.

Neutrinos

🪐 **Neutrinos are electrically neutral** subatomic particles that are produced in great numbers by nuclear reactions that take place inside stars.

🪐 **Neutrinos travel through space** at the speed of light in straight lines, and are only affected by two of the four fundamental forces – weak nuclear force and gravity (*see* Gravity and Mass).

▼ *The Super Kamiokande is a joint US-Japanese neutrino detector 1000 m underground in a mine near Hida, Japan. It began operation in 1996.*

- **Neutrinos interact very weakly** with other forms of matter, which allows them to travel through almost all objects, from the rocks of planets and moons to living things like humans.

- **Once thought to be 'ghost' particles** that had no mass, neutrinos do in fact have a very small mass.

- **The mass of neutrinos** was once believed to be one of the main components of dark matter. But it is now thought that neutrinos form only a small proportion of dark matter, being one of the forms of 'hot' dark matter.

- **Nuclear reactions in the Sun** are the main source of neutrinos that arrive at Earth. Supernovae, or exploding stars, are another main source.

- **Every second**, a finger-nail sized area on Earth has 60 billion neutrinos passing through it.

- **US astronomer R Davis Jnr** (1914–2006), who was awarded a Nobel Prize in 2002, was the first to detect neutrinos produced by the Sun. To make his discovery, Davis built a large steel tank deep underground and filled it with 600 tonnes of dry-cleaning fluid. He measured the reaction as neutrinos passed through the liquid.

- **There are three types of neutrino** – the electron neutrino, the muon neutrino, and the tau neutrino. They sometimes change from one type to another.

- **A team of scientists** using the Super Kamiokande detector in Japan, with a tank containing 45,000 tonnes of ultra-pure water, were the first to observe the transformation of a muon neutrino to a tau neutrino in 1998.

Life

Life is only known to exist on Earth. Our planet is suitable for life because of its gas atmosphere, surface water and moderately warm temperatures. Life probably began on Earth more than 3.5 billion years ago.

The first life-forms were probably bacteria that lived in very hot water around underwater volcanoes.

Some scientists believe that life's basic chemicals formed on Earth. Others think that they came from space, maybe on comets.

The panspermia theory says that life exists in many places in the Universe, spread by comets, meteoroids, asteroids and similar space bodies.

Basic organic chemicals, such as amino acids, have been detected in nebulae, meteorites and comets.

Huge lightning flashes may have caused big organic molecules to form on the Earth when it was young.

Saturn's icy moon, Titan, has evidence of organic (life) chemicals, as discovered by the Cassini–Huygens mission, which launched in 1997. Jupiter's moon, Europa, may have water below its surface, which could spawn life.

▶ *The surface of Mars has been explored by several landers and rovers, but no evidence for life has been found.*

▲ This artist's impression shows the Huygens probe plunging through the clouds in Titan's atmosphere in 2005, gathering information as it descends.

DID YOU KNOW?

On Earth, life exists everywhere in all conditions – hot, cold, wet and dry. However, no signs of life have been found anywhere else.

Extraterrestrials

🪐 **Extraterrestrial (ET) means** 'outside the Earth'.

🪐 **Some scientists believe** that ET or alien life could develop anywhere in the Universe where there is a flow of energy.

🪐 **Most scientists believe** that if there is ET life anywhere else in the Universe, it is probably based on organic chemistry, that is, the chemistry of carbon, as life on Earth is. An alternative is silicon.

▼ *People have reported spotting UFOs (Unidentified Flying Objects), such as so-called flying saucers, for more than 60 years.*

REC
4:3

- **If civilizations exist** elsewhere, they may be on planets circling other stars.

- **The Drake Equation** was proposed by astronomer Frank Drake (1930–) in 1961 to calculate how many civilizations there could be in our galaxy – the figure is millions.

- **Many stories and tales** exist of people seeing alien spacecraft or other UFOs, encountering aliens, or even being captured by them and visiting their craft or home world.

- **However there is no serious scientific proof** that any ET life-form has ever visited Earth.

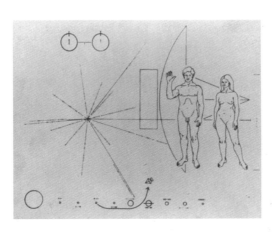

◄ The space probes Pioneer 10 and 11 carry metal panels with picture messages about life on Earth into deep space. If found by extraterrestrials, they would regard us as aliens.

SETI

- **The Search for Extraterrestrial Intelligence**, SETI, tries to detect signs of aliens or extraterrestrials (life-forms from places other than Earth).

- **The SETI Institute** aims to 'explore, understand and explain the origin, nature and prevalence of life in the Universe'. Its base is in Mountain View, California, US.

- **There have been various SETI projects** and campaigns for more than a century.

- **When radio waves** were discovered in the late 19th Century, some scientists suggested beaming them into space to communicate with beings on Mars.

- **The main search methods** used by SETI include various telescopes to detect purpose-made, non-natural patterns in electromagnetic waves.

- **This is because** electromagnetic waves all travel at the speed of light – the only practical way of covering the vast distances from (or to) any kind of extraterrestrial intelligence.

- **Monitoring all the wavelengths** and frequencies (numbers of waves per second), coming from all directions of space, is a gigantic task, however.

DID YOU KNOW?

Anyone can get involved in the search by lending their computer's processing time via the internet, using SETI@home.

▲ *Mars may once have had water lakes like this, that could have harboured some kinds of simple life-forms.*

🪐 **It is also difficult** to know which signals could be from extraterrestrial intelligence rather than natural sources such as the radio 'beeps' of pulsars.

🪐 **In 2015** the SETI Institute, along with famous supporters including Stephen Hawking, launched the Breakthrough Initiatives. These include renewed efforts to detect extraterrestrial messages using more and better equipment, and discussing the wisdom of sending our own messages into space.

Stars and galaxies

Stars

🪐 **Stars are giant balls of gas**, mainly hydrogen and helium.

🪐 **Nuclear reactions** in the heart of a star generate enormous energy, which the star sends out as heat, light and other forms of radiation, and various particles too.

🪐 **The heart or core of a star** reaches 15 million°C or more. A grain of sand this hot could kill someone 100 km away.

🪐 **The gas in stars** is in a special hot state called plasma, which is made of atoms stripped of electrons.

🪐 **In the core of a star**, hydrogen nuclei fuse (join together) to form helium. This nuclear reaction is called a proton-proton chain.

Large blue-white star

Medium-sized yellow star

Small red star

▲ *Large stars are hot and white, and smaller stars are cool and red. A large star can make energy faster and get much hotter than a smaller star. Medium-sized stars, such as our Sun, look yellow.*

Stars twinkle because they are seen through Earth's atmosphere where the air and dust affect their light rays.

Astronomers work out the size of a star from its brightness, colour, temperature and the various radiation it emits.

The size and brightness of a star depends on its mass – how much gas it is made of. The Sun is a small-medium star. The biggest stars have up to 200 times the Sun's mass, and the smallest ones about one tenth of its mass.

The coolest stars, such as Arcturus and Antares, glow reddest. Hotter stars are yellow and white. The hottest are blue-white, like Rigel and Zeta Puppis.

The blue supergiant Zeta Puppis has a surface temperature of 42,000°C, while blue-white supergiant Rigel's is 12,000°C.

▶ The globular swarm, or large cluster, of stars known as M80 (NGC 6093), is in the Milky Way galaxy, 32,000 light years from Earth. It contains hundreds of thousands of stars, attracted to each other by gravity.

Celestial sphere

- **Stars seem to move** across the sky as though they are on the inside of an imaginary giant ball. This concept is known as the celestial sphere.

- **Its northern extremity**, the North Celestial Pole, is directly above Earth's Geographic North Pole. Likewise the South Celestial Pole is directly above Earth's Geographic South Pole.

- **The celestial sphere seems to turn** on an axis that runs between its two poles, through Earth (although it is Earth that rotates).

- **There is a Celestial Equator** around the middle of the celestial sphere, just like the Equator on Earth's surface.

- **The positions of stars** on the celestial sphere are given by their declination (Dec.) and right ascension (R.A.).

- **Declination is like latitude**, up or down. It shows a star's position between the Celestial Pole and the Celestial Equator.

- **Right ascension is like longitude**, left or right. It shows how far a star is from the First Point of Aries.

- **The celestial sphere concept** does not include star distances.

- **There are several other systems** for pinpointing a star's position, such as the ecliptic and galactic systems.

- **The zenith** is the point on the sphere above a person's head as they look directly up into the night sky.

▶ *The celestial sphere is like a great ball dotted with stars, with the Earth in the middle. Its boundaries are imaginary but make it easy to locate stars and constellations. The zodiac is shown on the inset.*

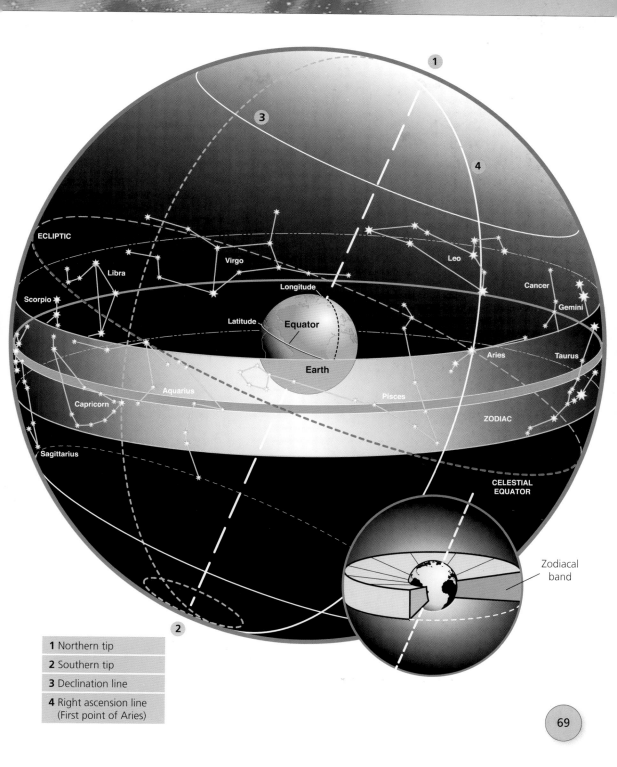

ECLIPTIC

Virgo

Libra

Leo

Scorpio

Cancer

Gemini

Longitude

Latitude

Equator

Aries

Taurus

Earth

Aquarius

Pisces

Capricorn

ZODIAC

Sagittarius

CELESTIAL
EQUATOR

Zodiacal
band

1 Northern tip

2 Southern tip

3 Declination line

4 Right ascension line
(First point of Aries)

Star names

Most of the brightest stars in the night sky were given individual names by the ancient Greeks. Arabic-speaking astronomers renamed many of these during the Middle Ages.

DID YOU KNOW?

Johann Bayer produced the first star atlas that included the entire sky in 1603.

Arcturus means 'bear warden' in Greek, and the star was given that name because it appears to follow the Great Bear across the sky.

The star Beta Orionis was named Rigel (which means 'the foot' in Arabic) because it forms one of the hunter's feet in the constellation of Orion.

Alpha Orionis has the name Betelgeuse (pronounced 'beetle-juice'), which comes from a mistaken translation of its original Arabic name Yad al-Jawza (which means 'the hand of Orion').

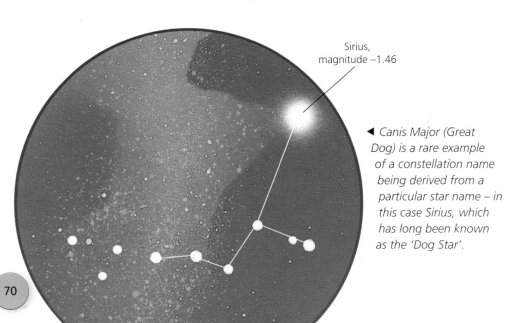

Sirius, magnitude −1.46

◄ Canis Major (Great Dog) is a rare example of a constellation name being derived from a particular star name – in this case Sirius, which has long been known as the 'Dog Star'.

▶ This 17th century map of the constellations shows that many were named after mythical people and gods, also real creatures.

🪐 **The constellation of Libra** was once known as the Scorpion's Claws. Consequently, the two brightest stars are Zubenelchemale ('Northern Claw') and Zubenelgenubi ('Southern Claw').

🪐 **In 1603**, the German astronomer Johan Bayer introduced the present system of designating the brightest stars in a constellation by the letters of the Greek alphabet.

🪐 **Variable stars have their own system**. They are designated by constellation in order of discovery in the sequence R, S, T, U, V, W, X, Y, Z. After Z the next variable star in the constellation is designated RR, and the next RS and so on.

🪐 **England's first Astronomer Royal**, John Flamsteed (1646–1719), preferred a different system in which all the visible stars in a constellation were given a number. Some stars, such as 61 Cygni, are still known by their Flamsteed numbers.

Star birth

🪐 **Medium-sized stars** last for about 10 billion years. Small stars may last for 200 billion years. Big stars have comparatively short, fierce lives of ten million years or less.

🪐 **Stars that begin life** in clouds of gas and dust are called nebulae.

🪐 **Inside nebulae**, gravity creates vast dark clumps called evaporating gaseous globules (EGGs). Each clump contains the beginnings of a family of stars.

🪐 **As gravity's attraction squeezes** these globules together, they shrink and form hot, spinning balls of gas and dust.

🪐 **Smaller clumps** do not get very hot, so they eventually fizzle out.

🪐 **If a larger clump** reaches 10 million°C in its core, hydrogen atoms begin to join together or fuse in nuclear reactions and the baby star or proto-star starts to glow.

🪐 **In a medium-sized star**, such as the Sun, the heat of burning hydrogen pushes gas out as fiercely as gravity pulls inwards, and the star becomes stable, giving out radiation at a steady rate.

◄ *In the centre of this massive galactic nebula is a cluster of young, bright stars.*

▼ *Stars are born and die all over the Universe. By looking at stars at different stages of their life, astronomers have learned about the stages of their existence.*

1 Clumps of gas in a nebula start to shrink into tight balls that will become stars

2 The gas spirals as it is pulled inwards. Any leftover gas and dust may form planets around the new star

3 Deep in its centre, the new star starts making energy, but it is still hidden by the cloud of dust and gas

4 The dust and gas are blown away and the shining star can be seen

73

Small stars

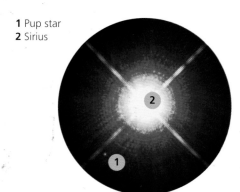 **Depending on their colour**, small stars of low brightness are called red, white, brown or black dwarves.

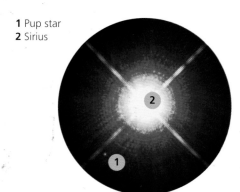 **Red dwarves are bigger** than the planet Jupiter, but smaller than the medium-sized star, the Sun. They glow faintly with less than 5 percent of the Sun's brightness.

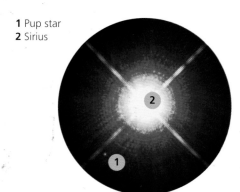 **No red dwarf can be seen** with the naked eye – not even the nearest star to the Sun, the red dwarf Proxima Centauri.

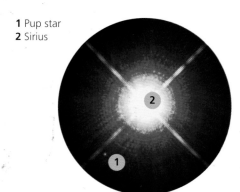 **White dwarves** are the last stage in the life of a medium-sized star. Although they are even smaller than red dwarves, they contain the same amount of matter as the Sun.

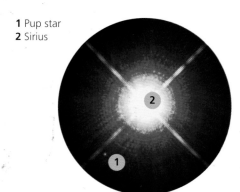 **The star 40 Eridani** is really three dwarf stars – a white dwarf and a red dwarf circling a small orange star, which can just be seen with the naked eye.

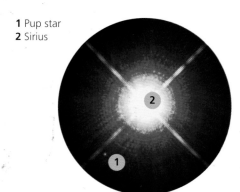 **Brown dwarves** are cool space objects, a little bigger than Jupiter. They formed in the same way as other stars, but were not big enough to start shining properly. They just glow very faintly with the heat left over from their formation.

1 Pup star
2 Sirius

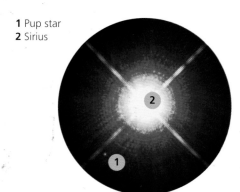

◀ *The night sky's brightest star, Sirius the Dog Star, has a white dwarf companion called the Pup Star.*

Black dwarves will be very small, cold, dead stars. They are either not big enough ever to start shining, or they will burn all their nuclear fuel and stop glowing.

▼ *Ejecting gas outwards, this planetary nebula is the closest example of the way a star evolves into a white dwarf.*

DID YOU KNOW?

The Universe is not yet old enough for black dwarves to have formed.

Giant stars

▼ Red giant stars expand and eject or 'throw off' matter in cloud-like layers. Our own Sun is about the right size to do this, probably in six or seven billion years, when it will have two-thirds of its current mass – and enlarge to swallow Earth and perhaps Mars.

▶ *The constellation Cygnus, the Swan, contains a group of giant blue stars including one of the brightest known, which is almost 100 times as big as the Sun.*

Giant stars are 10 to 100 times as big as the Sun, and 10 to 1000 times as bright.

Red giants are stars that have swollen 10 to 100 times their former size, as they reach their last stages and their outer gas layers cool and expand.

Giant stars have burned all their hydrogen, and so burn helium, fusing (joining) helium atoms to make carbon.

The biggest stars continue to swell after they become red giants. They then grow into supergiants.

Supergiant stars are up to 500 times as big as the Sun, with absolute magnitudes of −5 to −10.

Pressure in the centre of a supergiant is enough to fuse carbon atoms together to make the metallic chemical element iron.

Much of the iron in the Universe was made in the hearts of supergiant stars.

There is a limit to the brightness of supergiants, so they can be used as distance markers by comparing how bright they look from Earth to how bright they actually are.

Supergiant stars eventually collapse and explode as supernovae.

Star brightness

- **Star brightness is measured** on a scale of magnitude that was first devised in 150 BC by the Greek astronomer Hipparchus.

- **The brightest star** that Hipparchus could see was Antares, and he described it as magnitude 1. He described the faintest star he could see as magnitude 6.

- **Using telescopes and binoculars**, astronomers can now see much fainter stars than Hipparchus could.

- **The apparent or relative magnitude scale** describes how bright a star looks from Earth compared to other stars.

- **The further away a star is**, the dimmer it looks and the bigger its relative apparent magnitude is, regardless of how bright it really is.

- **Good binoculars show** apparent magnitude 9 stars, while a home telescope will show apparent magnitude 10 stars.

- **Brighter stars than Antares** have been identified with apparent magnitudes of less than 1, and even minus numbers. Betelgeuse averages 0.4, Vega 0.03, Alpha Centauri –0.27 and Canopus –0.72.

- **The brightest star visible** from Earth (excluding the Sun) is Sirius, the Dog Star, with a magnitude of –1.46.

- **A star's absolute magnitude** describes how bright a star actually is, seen from a standard distance of 32.6 light years, or 10 parsecs.

- **The star Rigel** is more than 200,000 times brighter than the Sun. However, as it is 850 light years away, it looks much dimmer.

- **Rigel's apparent magnitude** is 0.13, its absolute magnitude –7.9. This compares with –26.7 and 4.8 for the Sun.

BRIGHTEST STARS FROM EARTH	DISTANCE FROM EARTH	APPARENT MAGNITUDE
Our Sun	0.000,016 light years	-26.72
Sirius	8.6 light years	-1.46
Canopus	310 light years	-0.72
Alpha Centauri	4.37 light years	-0.27
Arcturus	36.7 light years	-0.05

DID YOU KNOW?
The Pistol Star, one of our galaxy's brightest, is absolute magnitude –10.8. But at 25,000 light years away its apparent magnitude is only 6.5.

▲ To estimate a star's magnitude, its brightness is compared to two stars with known magnitude – one star a little brighter and one a little dimmer.

H-R diagram

- **The Hertzsprung-Russell (H-R) diagram** was devised in about 1910 by Danish astronomer Ejnar Hertzsprung (1873–1967) and US astronomer Henry Russell (1877–1957).

- **An incredibly useful tool** in astronomy and space science, the H-R diagram is a 'scatter graph' that plots the temperature of stars against their brightness or magnitude.

- **The temperature of a star** is indicated by its colour. Cool stars are red or reddish-yellow, medium ones are yellow and hot stars burn white or blue.

- **Medium-sized stars** form a diagonal band called the main sequence across the middle graph.

- **The whiter and hotter a main sequence star is**, the brighter it shines. White stars and blue-white stars are usually bigger and younger.

- **The redder and cooler a star is**, the dimmer it glows. Cool red stars tend to be smaller and older.

- **Giant stars and white dwarf** stars lie to either side of the band of main sequence stars.

- **One use of the H-R diagram** is to show distance. If the star actually looks dimmer for its colour than it should be, it must be farther away from Earth.

DID YOU KNOW?
The great majority of main sequence stars will eventually become white dwarves.

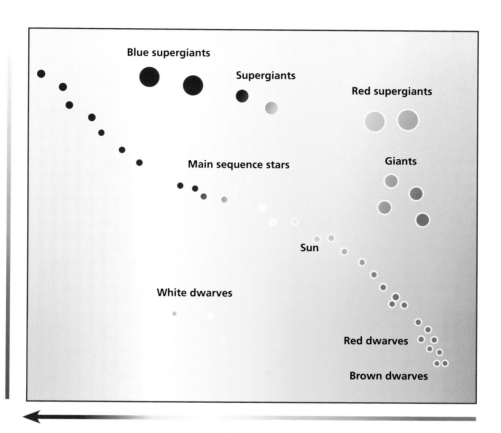

Increasing brightness

Blue supergiants

Supergiants

Red supergiants

Main sequence stars

Giants

Sun

White dwarves

Red dwarves

Brown dwarves

Increasing temperature

▲ By comparing a star's actual brightness, predicted by the H-R diagram, with how bright it looks from Earth, astronomers can work out how far away it is. The H-R diagram can also show the 'life' of a star. For example the Sun, currently in the main sequence, will in five or six billion years become a red giant, then eventually shrink into a white dwarf.

Binary and multiple stars

- **The Sun is alone in space**, but most stars are in groups of two or more.

- **Binaries are double stars** and there are various kinds. True binary stars are two stars that are held together by one another's gravity. Usually one is A and one B, such as Mira A, a red giant, and Mira B, a white dwarf.

▼ *The Alpha Centauri triple system consists of A (centre) and B (lower right), which orbit each other once every 80 years, plus the red dwarf C (not shown). A and B were first discerned as two stars in 1689 by French-born priest and astronomer Jean Richaud, who was working in Puducherry (Pondicherry), India.*

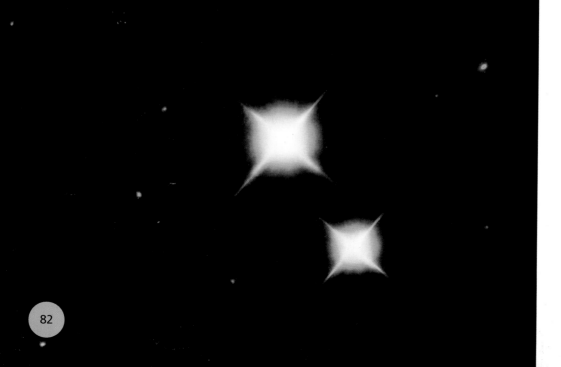

▼ *Many stars are binaries or multiples – two or more stars close together. Their motions depend on their sizes. The left image shows two similar stars following each other in circular orbit, while the right image shows a smaller star orbiting a large star.*

🌀 **Optical binaries** are not binaries at all. They are two stars that look as if they are together because they are in roughly the same line of sight when observed from Earth.

🌀 **Eclipsing binaries are true binary stars** that spin around in exactly the same line of sight from Earth, and keep blocking out each other's light.

🌀 **Spectroscopic binaries are true binaries** that spin so closely together that the only way of knowing that there are two stars is by their changes in colour.

🌀 **The star Epsilon**, in the constellation of Lyra, is called the Double Double because it is a pair of binaries.

🌀 **True multiple stars** have three (triple), four (quadruple) or more stars close together and are bound by their gravity.

🌀 **The closest stars to Earth** form a triple star system. Alpha Centauri A and B are Sun-sized yellow stars, grouped with a red dwarf, Proxima Centauri, which is one seventh the Sun's diameter.

Variable stars

🪐 **Stars that do not burn steadily** like the Sun, but flare up and down are called variable stars.

🪐 **Pulsating, or intrinsic, variables** are stars that physically expand and contract or otherwise vary in brightness. They include stars known as Cepheid variables and RR Lyrae variables.

🪐 **Cepheid variables** are big, bright stars that pulsate with energy, flaring up regularly every one to 50 days. They are predictable in brightness and make good distance markers.

🪐 **RR Lyrae variables** are yellow supergiant stars near the end of their life that flicker as their fuel runs down.

▼ *The spiral galaxy NGC 4603 – the most distant galaxy in which Cepheid variables have been discovered.*

► *The constellation of Cygnus contains a vanishing star.*

🪐 **Mira-type variables** are similar to Mira in Cetus, the Whale, and vary regularly over months or years.

🪐 **RV Tauri variables** are very unpredictable, flaring up and down over changing periods of time.

🪐 **Extrinsic variables** are usually steady-glowing stars that are actually eclipsing binaries – they seem to flare and dim when one star gets in the way of the other.

🪐 **The 'Demon Star'** is Algol in Perseus. It seems to burn fiercely for 59 hours, become dim, then flare up again ten hours later. It is really an eclipsing binary as part of a triple star system.

🪐 **The 'Vanishing Star'** is Chi in Cygnus, the Swan. It can be seen with the naked eye for a few months each year, but then becomes so dim that it cannot be seen, even with large amateur telescopes.

Exoplanets

- **Exoplanets** (extra-solar planets) are planets that orbit stars other than the Sun.

- **The first exoplanet** discovery was HD 114762b in 1989. It orbits the binary star HD 114762, 130 light years away in the constellation Coma Berenices.

- **Exoplanets** are usually named after their star with an added lower-case (small) letter such as a, b, c and so on.

- **Various telescopes** search for exoplanets, especially the 'planet-hunter' Kepler space observatory.

- **One way to detect** an exoplanet is to look for a regular slight dimming of the star, as seen from Earth, when the exoplanet passes in front of it on each orbit.

▼ These diagrams show the possible habitable or 'Goldilocks' zones (for Earth-like life) in green around three stars, along with zones that are too hot in red, and too cold in blue. At the top is a very hot blue-white star, in the middle a medium yellow Sun-like star, and at the bottom a cool star.

▲ *Kepler-186f is an Earth-size exoplanet that orbits its star, Kepler 186, in the habitable zone. There are also four other planets in orbit around the star, which is about half the mass of the Sun.*

Another method is to detect the slight 'wobble' in a star caused by the planet's gravity pulling on it during each orbit.

Kepler 452 is a star 1400 light years away in the Cygnus constellation, and is about as hot as the Sun.

In 2015 the Kepler space observatory found an exoplanet orbiting the star, later named Kepler 452b. This rocky planet is about the same distance from its star as Earth is from the Sun.

Kepler 452b may be in the habitable or 'Goldilocks' zone. This zone is the region around a star which (like the third bowl of porridge in the story *Goldilocks and the Three Bears*) is neither too hot nor too cold, in this case for liquid water to exist – and liquid water is essential for life as we know it.

Many thousands of exoplanets are known, with hundreds more found yearly.

Novae

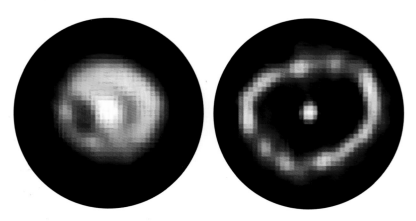

A nova (plural novae), which means 'new' in Latin, was the name given by early astronomers to the temporary appearance of a bright star in the sky.

In fact, a nova is a star that suddenly becomes up to a million times brighter than normal and then fades back to its original luminosity.

For a few weeks in 1901 the nova GK Persei outshone every other star in the sky except Sirius.

Some novae appear to fade within a few days, while others may take more than one year to return to their former dim state.

Novae are produced by binary stars where one of the pair is a white dwarf and the other is a larger and cooler star.

The white dwarf's gravity pulls hydrogen and other stellar material away from its companion star and this material builds up in layers around the surface of the white dwarf.

▲ *Two views of the nova Cygni 1992 obtained by the Hubble Faint Object Camera. The image on the right has been processed to reveal the shell of hot gas surrounding the 'parent' star.*

DID YOU KNOW?
The material ejected by a nova can travel through space at speeds of up to 1500 km/h.

- **As more material accumulates**, the temperature in the lowest layer steadily increases until it reaches about 20 million°C, at which point the hydrogen ignites.

- **The result is a massive nuclear explosion**, in effect a runaway chain reaction of nuclear fusion.

- **This explosion** blows away the upper layers of material in an expanding spherical cloud of glowing hot gas, and the process starts all over again.

- **Novae that have only** been observed to flare up once are known as classical novae. Those that have been seen more than once are known as recurrent novae.

- **In December 2013** in the constellation of Centaurus, Nova Centauri 2013 (also called V1369 Cen) flared up to an apparent magnitude, or brightness seen from Earth, of 3.3 – easily visible in the night sky to the unaided eye.

▶ *Nova Centauri 2013 appeared in the Southern Hemisphere skies, near the stars Beta Centauri (to its right) and the brighter Alpha Centauri (lower right). It lasted 2–3 weeks.*

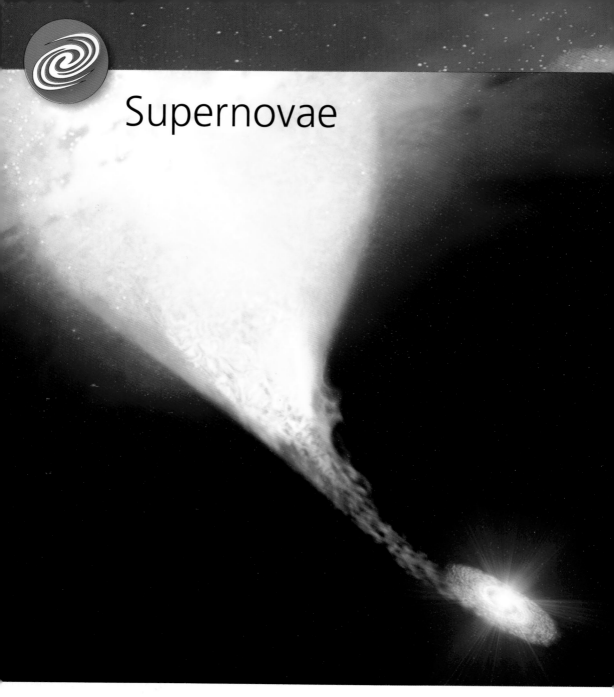

Supernovae

▲ *In this artist's view, one star of a binary (two-star) system is in the process of exploding as a supernova, having added some of its hydrogen gas to its companion blue star, which will endure. This type of 'survivor event' was first seen in 2004.*

- **A supernova** is the final, gigantic explosion of a supergiant star at the end of its life.

- **A supernova lasts** for just a week or so, but shines as brightly as a galaxy of 100 billion ordinary stars.

- **Supernovae occur when a supergiant star** uses up its hydrogen and helium fuel and shrinks. This boosts pressure in its core, enough to fuse heavy elements such as iron.

- **When iron begins to fuse** in its core, a star collapses at incredible speed – then rebounds in a mighty explosion.

- **Seen in 1987, SN (supernova) 1987A** was the first supernova viewable with the unaided eye since Kepler's 1604 sighting, now called SN 1604.

- **Supernova remnants** (leftovers) are the gigantic, cloudy shells of material swelling out from supernovae.

- **A supernova seen by Chinese** astronomers in AD 185 was thought to be such a bad omen that it sparked a revolution.

- **A dramatic supernova** seen by Chinese astronomers in 1054, now designated M1 or NGC 1952, created the Crab Nebula.

- **Many of the elements heavier** than iron are made in supernovae.

DID YOU KNOW?
Many of the elements that make up the human body were forged in supernovae.

Neutron stars

🪐 **Mainly made up of neutrons**, which are parts of an atom's nucleus, neutron stars are incredibly small, super-dense stars with a solid crust made of iron and similar elements.

🪐 **Although neutron stars** weigh as much as the Sun, they are just 20 km across on average.

🪐 **A tablespoon-full of a neutron star** would weigh about one million tonnes.

🪐 **Neutron stars form** from the central core of a star that has died in a supernova explosion.

🪐 **To produce a neutron star**, a star must be more than 1.4 times as massive as a medium-sized star, such as the Sun. This is known as the Chandrasekhar limit.

🪐 **A star more than three times** as massive as the Sun would collapse beyond a neutron star to form a black hole. This is called the Oppenheimer-Volkoff limit.

🪐 **The first evidence** of neutron stars came when pulsars (rapidly-spinning neutron stars) were discovered in the 1960s.

🪐 **Some stars giving out X-rays**, such as Hercules X-1, are neutron stars. The X-rays come from nearby stars as material is squeezed on to their surfaces by their gravity.

🪐 **Neutron stars have very powerful magnetic fields**, billions of times stronger than Earth's, which stretch the atoms out into frizzy 'whiskers' on the star's surface.

▲ The blue dot in the centre of this supernova explosion is probably a neutron star. Neutron stars are tiny, super-dense stars that form when a giant star's core collapses within seconds under the huge force of its own immense gravity.

Neutron star

Pulsars

🪐 **A pulsar is a neutron star** that spins rapidly, beaming out regular pulses of radio waves.

🪐 **The first pulsar** was detected by Cambridge astronomer, Jocelyn Bell Burnell (1943–), in 1967.

🪐 **At first, astronomers thought** the regular pulses might be signals from aliens, and pulsars were jokingly called LGMs (Little Green Men).

🪐 **Most pulsars send** their radio pulse about once a second. The slowest pulse every 10 seconds or more, and the fastest every 1.4 milliseconds, that is, about 715 times per second.

🪐 **As it gets older**, the pulse rate of a pulsar usually slows down.

🪐 **The Crab pulsar** slows by a millionth of a second a day.

🪐 **More than 1500 pulsars** are now known, but there may be 200,000 active in the Milky Way.

🪐 **Pulsars probably result** from a supernova explosion – that is why most are found in the flat disc of the Milky Way, where supernovae occur.

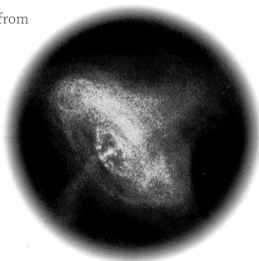

▶ *The Crab Nebula is the remnants of a stellar explosion. In this image, taken by the Chandra X-Ray Observatory, the central pulsar is clearly shown.*

▲ *Pulsar PSR B1257+12, discovered in 1992, has three planets circling it. The pulsar's magnetic fields are shown as a blue glow.*

🪐 **Pulsars are not found** in the same place as supernovae because they form after the debris from the explosion has spread into space.

🪐 **Some pulsars emit X-rays**, such as Centaurus X-3 in the constellation Centaurus, confirmed in 1971.

95

Stellar clusters

● **A stellar cluster** is a group of stars (a stellar system) where the constituent stars are located much more closely together than the surrounding stars, but not close enough to be multiple stars.

● **There are two distinct types of stellar cluster** – open clusters and globular clusters.

● **Open clusters contain** between a few hundred and several thousand fairly young stars, and they are mainly located in the same plane (ecliptic) as the spiral arms of the galaxy.

▼ *A telescope reveals that the Pleiades cluster contains many more stars than the bright stars that have given it the popular name 'Seven Sisters'.*

- **Most open clusters** are less than 500 million years old, and in some clusters the stars are so young (only a few million years old) that they are still embedded in the clouds from which they emerged.

- **The most famous** open cluster is the Pleiades, which is also known as the Seven Sisters – although there are nine stars in the cluster that are visible to the unaided eye.

- **Globular clusters are much bigger** than open clusters and contain up to one million stars. They are also much older, many dating back more than 10 billion years.

- **The globular cluster M92** has an estimated age of more than 13 billion years, making it almost as old as the Universe itself.

- **In our galaxy**, the Milky Way, globular clusters are mainly located above and below the galactic plane. They are also concentrated around the galactic centre in a spherical cloud that is called the galactic halo.

- **Stars in globular clusters** are sometimes described as metal-poor because they were formed so long ago, before the Universe contained many atoms of heavier, denser metallic elements.

- **Younger stars**, like our Sun and the stars in open clusters, are considered to be metal-rich.

Nebulae

- **Any fuzzy patch of light** in the night sky was once called a nebula. Nowadays, many of these are known to be galaxies.

- **A nebula is now defined** as a gigantic cloud of gas and dust.

- **Glowing nebulae** give off a dim, red light as the hydrogen gas in them is heated by radiation from nearby stars.

- **The Orion Nebula** (M42 or NGC 1976) is a glowing nebula just visible to the naked eye in the Orion constellation.

- **Reflection nebulae** have no light. They can only be seen because starlight shines off the dust in them.

- **Dark nebulae not only have no light** of their own, they also soak up all light. They can only be seen as patches of darkness blocking out light from the stars behind them.

- **The Horsehead Nebula in Orion** is a well known dark nebula. As its name suggests, it is shaped like a horse's head.

- **Planetary nebulae** are thin rings of gas cloud thrown out by dying stars. Despite their name, they have nothing to do with planets.

- **The Ring Nebula in Lyra** (M57, NGC 6720) is a well known planetary nebula.

◄ One of the most complex nebulae to be discovered is the Cat's Eye Nebula (NGC 6543).

▶ The Trifid Nebula (M20, NGC 6514) glows as hydrogen and helium gas within is heated by radiation from stars.

Galaxies

🪐 **Giant groups of millions** or even trillions of stars are called galaxies. Our own local galaxy, containing the Solar System, is called the Milky Way.

🪐 **There are more than 175 billion** galaxies in the known Universe, and possibly more to be discovered.

🪐 **The three galaxies** most visible to the unaided eye from Earth (besides the Milky Way) are the Large and Small Magellanic clouds, and the Andromeda Galaxy.

🪐 **In 1923**, astronomers realized that galaxies are huge star groups. They are vast but so far away that they look like fuzzy clouds.

🪐 **Galaxies are often found** in groups called clusters. One cluster may contain hundreds of galaxies.

🪐 **Spiral galaxies** are spinning galaxies with a dense core and spiralling arms.

🪐 **Irregular galaxies** have no obvious shape. They may have formed from the debris of galaxies that crashed into each other.

🪐 **Elliptical galaxies are vast**, old, egg-shaped galaxies, made up of as many as a trillion stars.

🪐 **Barred spiral galaxies** have just two arms. These are linked across the middle of the galaxy by a bar from which they trail.

DID YOU KNOW?

About 2400 years ago, Democritus of ancient Greece suggested the band we call the Milky Way (our galaxy) was composed of countless distant stars.

▶ *There are various sizes, types and shapes of galaxies in the Universe. These are some of the main shapes, but there are many others.*

Spiral

Irregular

Elliptical

The Milky Way

🪐 **The faint, hazy band** of light that can be seen stretching right across the night sky is the Milky Way.

🪐 **With binoculars**, thousands of the billions of stars that make up the Milky Way can be seen.

🪐 **The Milky Way** is the view of our galaxy from Earth. We are inside its disc, looking through its thickness.

🪐 **Our galaxy is 100,000 or more light years** across and 1000 light years thick. It is made up of at least 100 billion stars, and possibly five times that many.

🪐 **All the stars are arranged** in a spiral with a bulge in the middle. The bulge is about 20,000 light years across and 3000 light years thick, with very old stars and little dust or gas.

🪐 **The Sun is just one** of the billions of stars, about halfway from the centre on one arm of the spiral, the Orion Arm.

🪐 **The Milky Way** is whirling rapidly, spinning our Sun and its Solar System around at 800,000 km/h.

🪐 **Once every 220 million years**, the Solar System and all local stars complete one orbit around the Milky Way centre – a journey of 170,000 light years.

🪐 **At the centre of the Milky Way** is an immensely powerful source of radio energy, Sagittarius A*. It may well be a supermassive black hole.

▶ *The arms at the edge of the Milky Way contain many young, bright stars, while the middle is dust and gas.*

1	Outer Arm
2	Perseus Arm
3	The Sun
4	Orion Spur
5	Sagittarius Arm
6	Far 3kpc Arm
7	Near 3kpc Arm
8	Norma Arm
9	Scutum-Centaurus Arm

Local Group

🪐 **In 1936**, the term Local Group was coined by Edwin Hubble to describe the cluster of nearby galaxies to which the Milky Way galaxy belongs.

🪐 **More than 50 galaxies** have been identified as belonging to the Local Group, more than half of which have only been discovered during the last 30 years. All of the galaxies in the Local Group interact gravitationally.

🪐 **In addition to the Milky Way**, there are two other spiral galaxies in the Local Group: the Andromeda Galaxy (M31) and the smaller Triangulum or Pinwheel Galaxy (M33). Our galaxy and Andromeda together contain over 90 percent of the Group's mass.

🪐 **All of the other members** of the local group are dwarf galaxies, of which the best known are the Large Magellanic Cloud and the Small Magellanic Cloud.

🪐 **Some of the dwarf galaxies** are so dim that their brightness is less than that of the night sky, making them difficult to detect.

🪐 **The Milky Way** has more than 15 dwarf galaxies that orbit around it in the same way that moons orbit around a planet.

🪐 **The Sagittarius dwarf galaxy** is so close that it is in the process of being absorbed into the Milky Way.

🪐 **The Local Group** is also interacting with nearby groups of galaxies. It has stretched the nearby loose Sculptor Group so much that there is no gap of intergalactic space between them.

🪐 **On an even larger scale**, the Local Group is slowing moving towards the larger Local or Laniakea Supercluster.

DID YOU KNOW?

One of the smallest Local Group galaxies is Leo T. It is suspected of having an unusually high proportion of dark matter.

▲ *The Large Magellanic Cloud is located 162,000 light years from Earth. It is affected by the gravity of our Milky Way galaxy and in turn its gravitational force is distorting its close neighbour, the Small Magellanic Cloud.*

105

Quasars

🪐 **The most intense light sources** in the Universe, quasars are no bigger than the Solar System, yet they glow more brightly than 100 galaxies, like the Milky Way.

🪐 **Quasars are the most distant** known objects in the Universe. Even the nearest is a billion light years away.

🪐 **Quasar is short for** Quasi-Stellar (star-like) Radio Source. This comes from the fact that the first quasars were detected by the strong radio signals they give out, and also because quasars are so small and bright that at first people thought they looked like stars.

🪐 **Less than 10 percent** of the 100,000-plus quasars now known actually beam out radio signals.

🪐 **One of the brightest quasars**, 3C 273, is 2.44 billion light years away. It was the first recorded quasar in 1959. Its mass is 900 million times that of the Sun and it shines 4000 billion times more brightly than the Sun.

🪐 **Some quasars are so far away** that we see them as they were when the Universe was still in its infancy. An example is the colossally bright quasar, ULAS J1120+0641, 13 billion light years away – one of the most distant objects ever detected. It formed less than one billion years after the Universe itself began.

🪐 **Quasars are at the centre** of 'active galaxies'. Their energy comes from a black hole at their core, which ferociously draws in matter.

🪐 **The energy given out** by this matter heading towards the black hole is radiated as heat, light, radio and other waves, which have enough power to travel across the Universe.

▲ *This artist's impression depicts an active quasar. Winds in the outer regions of the quasar contain dust particles.*

Black holes

🪐 **When a star or galaxy** of a certain size becomes so dense that it collapses under the pull of its own gravity, it becomes a black hole.

🪐 **Gravity is so strong** in a black hole that it sucks in everything, including all matter, radiation and other energy.

🪐 **This immense gravity shrinks** the black hole to an unimaginably small, dense point called a singularity, where vast amounts of matter and energy are squeezed into almost nothing.

🪐 **Around the singularity** is the 'place of no return' for matter and energy falling into the black hole, called the event horizon.

🪐 **Nothing can leave a black hole**, including light – so it is 'black'.

🪐 **However one theory** involving quantum effects says that a certain kind of energy could be emitted from a black hole, called Hawking radiation after the famous scientist Stephen Hawking (1942–).

🪐 **A stellar black hole**, formed from one collapsed star, has a mass of about 10 to 100 times that of the Sun.

🪐 **Supermassive black holes** with millions – even billions – of stars may exist at the heart of every galaxy.

🪐 **Around the singularity**, gravity is so intense that space-time is bent into a funnel.

🪐 **Matter spiralling into the funnel** and towards the black hole is torn apart and glows so brightly that it creates the most luminous objects in the Universe – quasars.

🪐 **The swirling gases** around a black hole turn it into an electrical generator, spouting jets containing electrons that surge billions of kilometres out into space.

◀ *The gravity of a black hole is so strong that nothing can escape, not even light. Planets, stars, gas and dust are pulled into the hole.*

Event horizon

- **A black hole** is centred on a singularity – a point where gigantic amounts of matter and energy, perhaps the same as in millions of stars, are squeezed into almost nothing.

- **The event horizon** around the black hole can be imagined as the 'place of no return'.

- **At the event horizon**, matter and energy (such as light) falling into the black hole must continue and can never escape.

- **The horizon** can be explained as the boundary where the gravitational pull of the black hole becomes greater than the speed of light.

- **Another description** is that the black hole's immense gravity bends or warps space-time so much, that as an object or a form of energy (like light) approaches closer and closer, more and more of its possible directions of movement lead to the black hole.

- **Eventually at the event horizon**, space is so warped that all possible directions now go into the black hole.

- **Almost any object**, if squashed small and dense enough, could become a black hole.

- **The object's size** at the stage where an event horizon forms and the object can become a black hole, is called its Schwarzschild radius. If the Earth was squeezed into its Schwarzschild radius, about 2 cm across, it would gain an event horizon and continue collapsing into a black hole.

- **In reality**, only stars larger than three times the mass of the Sun have enough gravity to cause their own collapse in this way.

▼ *The warping of space-time is often shown as a curved net or twisted grid. It shows how space itself bends so that a line is both straight and not straight.*

The Solar System

The Solar System

The Solar System consists of the Sun and all the objects orbiting within its gravitational field. It extends to the edge of the vast area known as the Oort Cloud.

There are eight planets in the Solar System. The four inner rocky planets are Mercury, Venus, Earth and Mars. The four outer gas planets are Jupiter, Saturn, Uranus and Neptune.

▼ *This illustration of the Solar System, with part of the Sun in the foreground, shows all the planets, although the distances between them have been greatly compressed.*

1 Mercury	**5** Jupiter	
2 Venus	**6** Saturn	
3 Earth	**7** Uranus	
4 Mars	**8** Neptune	

Sun

🪐 **The planets follow elliptical orbits** around the Sun and they all lie in the same plane, which is known as the solar ecliptic.

🪐 **The inner and outer planets** are separated by the Main Asteroid Belt, which contains many thousands of asteroids, with more than 60 orbiting Saturn.

🪐 **It takes light** over four hours to travel from the Sun to outermost planet Neptune.

🪐 **All the planets**, with the exception of Mercury and Venus, have at least one moon. Altogether there are more than 150 planetary moons in the Solar System, with over 50 orbiting Saturn.

🪐 **Pluto used to be considered a planet**, but in 2006 it was officially designated as a dwarf planet, along with the asteroid Ceres and various Kuiper Belt objects (KBOs).

🪐 **The Kuiper Belt** is a disc-shaped region of space that is 30–50 AU (Astronomical Units) from the Sun. It contains numerous orbiting objects, some over 1000 km in diameter.

🪐 **The Oort Cloud is** a spherical region of space between about 2000 and 100,000 AU from the Sun. It contains millions of comets.

🪐 **The outer edge of the Oort Cloud**, which is the edge of the Solar System, is almost halfway to the nearest star, Alpha Centauri – which may well be surrounded by its own comet cloud.

115

The Sun

🌑 **A medium-sized yellow star**, the Sun is a fiery ball of gas that measures 1,392,700 km across – 109 times the diameter of Earth.

🌑 **Even though the Sun** is made almost entirely of hydrogen and helium, the lightest gases in the Universe, it weighs 2000 trillion trillion tonnes – about 300,000 times as much as Earth.

🌑 **The Sun's interior** is heated by nuclear fusion reactions to temperatures of more than 15 million°C.

🌑 **Energy is produced in the central core** and very slowly works its way outwards through a thick layer of gases. In the outer layer, hot gas rises to the surface where heat and light escape into space.

🌑 **The heat from the Sun's interior** erupts on the surface in patches called granules, and as gigantic arcs of hot gases called solar prominences.

🌑 **The Sun gets hot** because it is so big that the pressure in its core is tremendous – enough to force the nuclei of hydrogen atoms to fuse (join together) to make helium atoms.

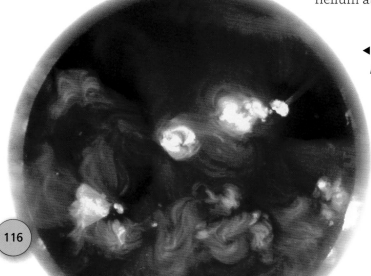

◄ This artificially coloured photo was taken by a satellite and shows the Sun's surface to be a turbulent mass of flames and tongues of hot gases – very different from the even, yellowish ball we see from Earth.

▶ *A cutaway of the Sun shows its layers, and the Solar and Heliospheric Observatory (SOHO) spacecraft, which spent two years gathering information about the Sun.*

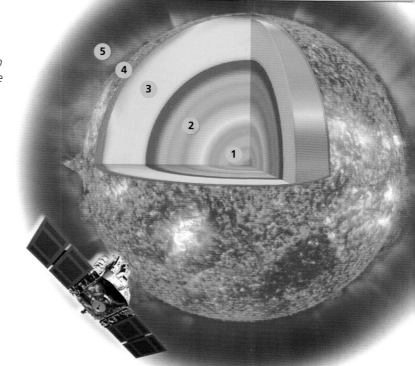

1 Core

2 Radiative zone

3 Convective zone

4 Photosphere

5 Chromosphere

🪐 **This nuclear fusion** reaction releases huge amounts of energy.

🪐 **Halfway between its core** and its surface, the Sun is as dense as water. Closer to the surface, it becomes as dense as air.

🪐 **Nuclear fusion reactions** in the Sun's core convert five million tonnes of gas into energy every second, but the energy takes ten million years to reach the surface.

DID YOU KNOW?
The Sun has been shining for over 4.5 billion years. Its current surface temperature is about 6000°C.

Sunspots

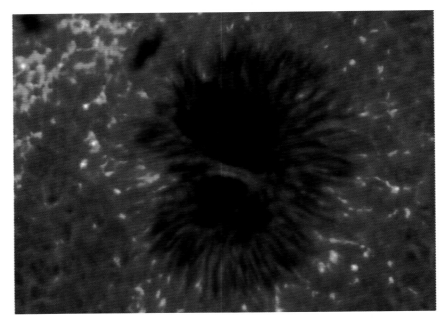

▲ *Infrared photographs reveal the dark sunspots that appear on the surface of the Sun.*

Dark spots on the Sun's photosphere (surface) are called sunspots. They are 1500°C cooler than the rest of the surface.

The dark centre of a sunspot is the umbra, the coolest part of a sunspot. Around it is the lighter penumbra.

Sunspots appear in groups that seem to move across the Sun over two weeks, as the Sun rotates. Some last less than a day.

The number of sunspots peaks every 11 years on average, varying from 9 to 14 years. This is the solar or sunspot cycle.

The last sunspot maximum was in 2013–2014.

🪐 **When sunspots are at their maximum**, Earth's weather may be warmer and stormier.

🪐 **Long-term sunspot cycles** last between 80 and 200 years.

🪐 **Observations of the Sun** by satellites such as Nimbus-7, showed that less heat reaches Earth from the Sun when sunspots are at a minimum.

DID YOU KNOW?

The SOHO satellite, launched in 1995, has revealed whirlpools of gases beneath sunspots.

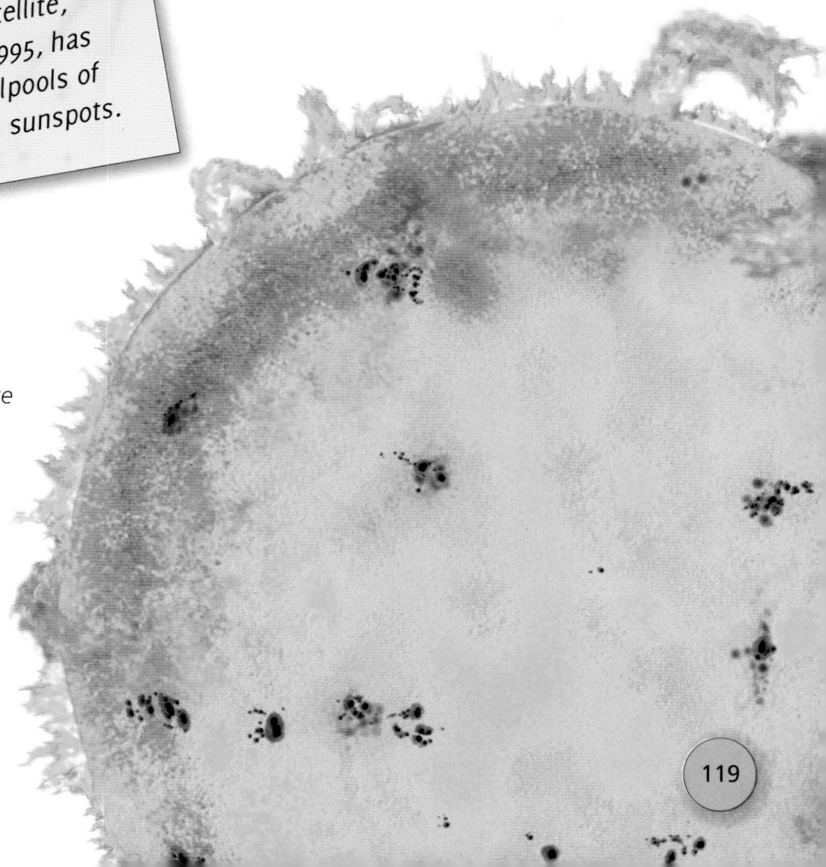

▶ Sunspots on the surface of the Sun are caused by areas of intense magnetic fields.

119

Solar eruptions

Solar flares are sudden eruptions on the Sun's surface. They flare up in just a few minutes, then take more than half an hour to die away again.

▼ Solar prominences can loop as far as 200,000 km out from the Sun's surface.

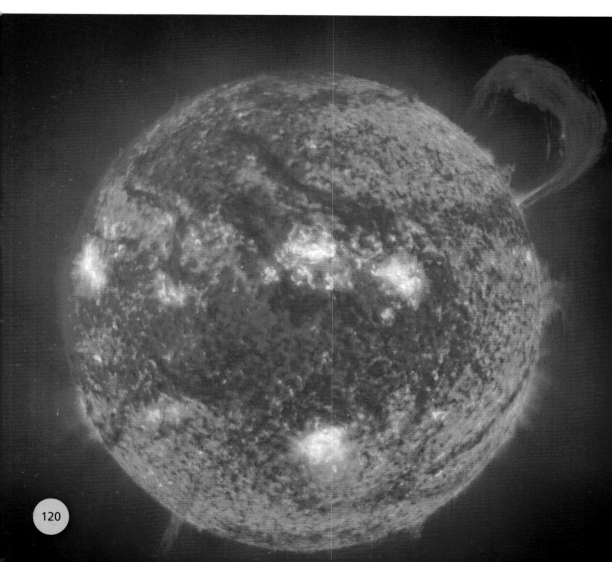

- **Solar flares reach temperatures** of 10 million°C and have the energy of billions of nuclear explosions.

- **As well as heat and radiation**, solar flares also send out streams of charged particles.

- **The solar wind is the stream** of charged particles that shoots out from the Sun in all directions at speeds of over one million km/h. It reaches Earth in several days, but also blows far throughout the Solar System.

- **Every second**, the solar wind carries away over one million tonnes of charged particles from the Sun.

- **Earth is shielded** from the lethal effects of the solar wind by its own magnetic field.

- **Solar prominences** are gigantic arcs of hot hydrogen that sometimes spout out from the Sun. They last from a few days to several weeks, and can reach temperatures of 10,000°C.

- **Coronal mass ejections** (CMEs) are gigantic eruptions of charged particles (protons and electrons) from the Sun, creating gusts in the solar wind that set off magnetic storms on Earth.

- **CMEs occur several times daily** when the solar or sunspot cycle is at its peak, but only once a week in between.

- **Magnetic storms** are massive hails of charged particles that hit Earth every few years or so, setting the atmosphere buzzing with electricity.

Solar changes

🪐 **The Sun is about 4.6 billion years old** and halfway through its life – as a medium-sized star it will probably live for around 11 billion years. Over the next few billion years, the Sun will brighten and swell until it is twice as bright and 50 percent bigger.

🪐 **In five billion years**, the Sun's hydrogen fuel will have burned out, and its core will start to shrink.

🪐 **As its core shrinks**, the rest of the Sun will swell up and its surface will become cooler and redder. It will be a red giant star.

🪐 **Earth will have burned** out long before the Sun is big enough to expand so much it completely swallows the planet.

🪐 **The Sun will end** as a white dwarf (the last stage in the life of a medium-sized star).

🪐 **Between 1645 and 1715**, few sunpots were seen on the Sun – this period is called the Maunder minimum. At that time Earth experienced an ice age known as the Little Ice Age, due to less heat from the Sun.

🪐 **More of the chemical carbon-14** is made on Earth when the Sun is less active. The carbon-14 is absorbed by trees, which means scientists can track changes in solar activity in the past by measuring carbon-14 in old wood.

🪐 **The SOHO** spacecraft is stationed between the Earth and the Sun. It monitors the Sun and changes in solar activity.

▶ *The Sun seems to burn steadily, although its brightness does vary very slightly over decades. Over the next five billion years there will be a long-term trend for it to burn more ferociously.*

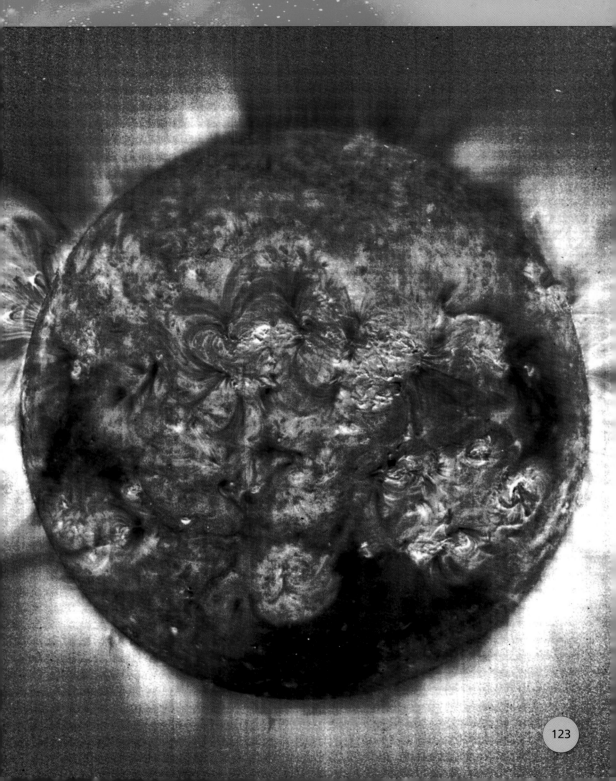

Planets

- **Planets are large globe-shaped objects** that orbit a star. Their gravity and rotation are powerful enough to make them spherical.

- **A planet has no other** appreciably large objects nearby, sharing its orbital zone or interfering with its gravity, except for any the planet dominates by its own gravity, like moons.

- **Most planets begin life** at the same time as their star, forming from the leftover clouds of gas and dust.

- **Planets are never** more than about five percent of the mass of the Sun. If they were bigger, they would be stars.

- **The Solar System's largest planet**, Jupiter, would need to have been 70–100 times more massive to begin nuclear fusion and become a very small star.

- **The Sun contains 99.86 percent** of the total mass in the Solar System. The planets only make up 1/2500th of the Solar System's mass.

- **Terrestrial planets** have a surface made of solid rock. Gas planets do not have a solid surface, just cloud, although some may have a core of dense liquid, semi-liquid or even solid.

- **The Solar System** has eight planets. Pluto was the ninth, but it is very small and is now classified as a dwarf planet (planetoid).

- **Thousands of planets** have been detected orbiting stars other than the Sun. These are called extra-solar planets or exoplanets.

▲ *Probes, such as the Hubble Space Telescope, are able to give scientists a more detailed view of the planets. Here, on the lower right, the Hubble has detected a storm on Mars.*

125

Moons

▼ *Enceladus orbits about 240,000 km from Saturn. It is a very active moon with jets and geysers of water vapour and other gases, crystals and various frozen particles. It probably has a hidden ocean of liquid water under the surface.*

- **Moons are the natural satellites** of planets. Most are small rock globes or lumps that continually orbit the planet, held in place by the planet's gravity.

- **There are more than 150 known planetary moons** in the Solar System, and more orbiting dwarf planets and asteroids.

- **Every planet in the Solar System** has a moon, apart from Mercury and Venus, the two planets nearest to the Sun.

- **New moons are frequently discovered**, as new space probes study the distant planets in more detail, and as the distance we can see using telescopes increases due to technological improvements – especially space observatories.

- **Several moons have atmospheres**, including Saturn's moon Titan, Jupiter's Io, and Neptune's Triton.

- **Jupiter's moon Ganymede** is the largest moon in the Solar System, measuring more than 5260 km across – half as wide again as Earth's Moon.

- **Second largest** is Saturn's moon Titan, at 5160 km in diameter. Icy cold, Titan is the only moon with a thick atmosphere of nitrogen gas.

- **The smallest moons** are icy lumps just one or 2 km across, rather like asteroids.

- **Saturn's moon Iapetus** is very pale on one side and almost black on the other.

- **Saturn's moon Enceladus** is only 500 km across, and its icy surface reflects almost all the sunlight.

Years

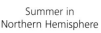
Summer in
Northern Hemisphere

🪐 **A year is the time taken** for a planet to go around, or orbit, its star once.

🪐 **An Earth calendar year is roughly this time** – Earth takes 365 days to travel around the Sun.

🪐 **However Earth actually takes 365.242 days** to orbit the Sun. This is called a solar or tropical year.

🪐 **To compensate for the missing 0.242 days**, the Western calendar adds an extra day in February every fourth (leap) year.

🪐 **When measured by the stars**, not the Sun, Earth takes 365.25636 days to go round the Sun. This is because the Sun also moves a little, relative to the stars. This is called the sidereal (star) year.

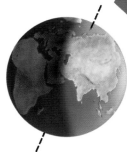

🪐 **Earth's perihelion** is the day its elliptical orbit brings it closest to the Sun – 3 January.

🪐 **Earth's aphelion** is the day in its orbit it is farthest from the Sun – 4 July.

🪐 **The planet with the shortest year** is Mercury, which speeds around the Sun in just 88 Earth days.

🪐 **Neptune is the planet with the longest year**. It takes 164.8 Earth years to orbit the Sun.

🪐 **The planet with the year** closest to the length of Earth's is Venus. A Venusian year lasts 225 Earth days.

▼ *The Earth orbits the Sun as though on a flat surface called the ecliptic plane. The planet's axis of rotation (the line around which it spins) is not at right angles to this, but 'leans' at 23.5°. This creates the different seasons.*

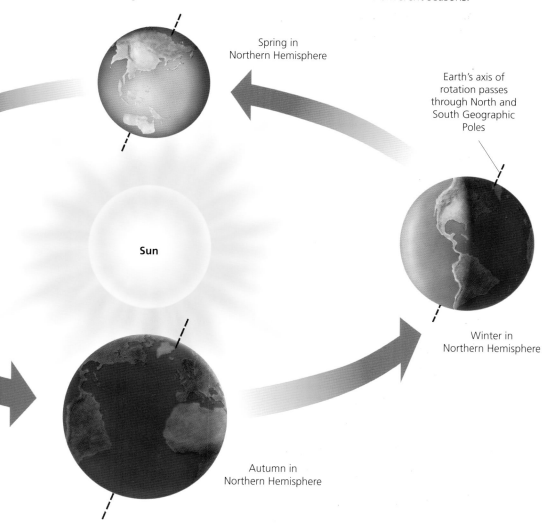

Spring in
Northern Hemisphere

Earth's axis of
rotation passes
through North and
South Geographic
Poles

Sun

Winter in
Northern Hemisphere

Autumn in
Northern Hemisphere

Day and night

- **A full day** (daytime plus night-time) is the time taken for a planet or similar space object to spin around once on its axis.

- **We are most familiar with Earth's day**, which is approximately 24 hours.

- **Earth turns eastwards** – this means that the Sun rises in the east, as each part of the world spins round to face it.

- **As Earth turns**, the stars come back to the same place in the night sky every 23 hours, 56 minutes and 4.09 seconds. This is a sidereal day.

- **It takes 24 hours** for the Sun to come back to the same place in Earth's daytime sky. This is the solar day, and it is slightly longer than the sidereal day because Earth moves about one degree farther around the Sun each day.

- **For each planet**, the length of day depends on how fast it takes to spin or rotate once, and sometimes its speed in orbit.

- **Mercury spins** once in every 58.6 Earth days, but its solar day is 176 Earth days because its orbit is near the Sun.

- **A day on Jupiter** lasts less than ten Earth hours because Jupiter spins so fast.

- **A day on Mars** is 24.6 Earth hours.

DID YOU KNOW?
A day on the Moon lasts nearly one Earth month.

▼ *When it is daylight on the half of Earth facing towards the Sun, it is night on the half of Earth facing away from it. As Earth rotates, the day and night halves shift gradually around the world.*

Solar calendar

🪐 **As Earth's orbit** around the sun is on a tilted axis, the Sun appears to gradually rise and fall in the sky during the year. This effect causes the sun to sometimes be visible at midnight at high latitudes near the poles.

🪐 **A solstice** (Greek for 'sun stop') is the day on which the Sun is at its highest or lowest for any midday during the year. The two yearly solstices are often called midsummer and midwinter.

🪐 **The northern summer solstice**, which occurs on 21 June, marks the Sun's most northerly extension above the Equator. At noon on 21 June the Sun is directly overhead at the Tropic of Cancer.

🪐 **The northern winter solstice**, which occurs on 21 December, marks the Sun's most southerly extension below the Equator. At noon on 21 December the Sun is directly overhead at the Tropic of Capricorn.

🪐 **An equinox** (which means 'equal night') marks both the time and place at which the Sun crosses the Equator. During an equinox, everywhere on the planet has exactly 12 hours of daylight and 12 hours of darkness.

🪐 **The vernal (spring) equinox** occurs around 21 March each year, and marks when the Sun crosses the Equator from south to north.

🪐 **The vernal equinox,** along with Aries, is used as the zero point R.A. in the celestial co-ordinate system, which specifies star positions (see Celestial sphere).

🪐 **On 23 September** each year, the autumn equinox occurs, which marks the Sun crossing the Equator from north to south.

◄ *Our understanding of the close link between astronomy and the calendar goes back a long way. Some of the standing stones at Stonehenge in England (built before 2000 BC) are aligned with the position of the rising Sun at the summer solstice.*

133

Atmosphere

🪐 **The gases held around a planet** or other large space object by its gravity make up its atmosphere.

🪐 **Every planet in the Solar System** has an atmosphere.

🪐 **Each atmosphere** is very different. Earth's atmosphere is the only one that humans can breathe.

🪐 **Atmospheres are not fixed**, but can change rapidly.

🪐 **Moons are generally too small** and their gravity is too weak to have an atmosphere. However, some moons have one, including Saturn's huge moon Titan.

🪐 **The primordial (earliest) atmospheres** came from the cloud of gas and dust surrounding the young Sun.

🪐 **If Earth and the other rocky planets** had primordial atmospheres, they were stripped away by solar wind.

🪐 **Earth's present atmosphere** was first formed from gases pouring out of volcanoes. It has since evolved greatly, becoming enriched with oxygen from plant activity.

🪐 **The atmosphere of Mars** is similar to that of Venus, made mainly of carbon monoxide, but it is much sparser or thinner than that of Venus.

🪐 **Jupiter's atmosphere** is partly primordial, but it has been altered by the Sun's radiation, and the planet's own internal heat and lightning storms.

▶ *In 2005 the lander Huygens floated down through the hazy atmosphere of Saturn's moon Titan, which consists almost entirely of nitrogen with some methane.*

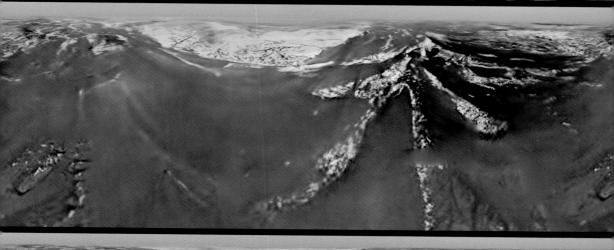

DID YOU KNOW?

The oxygen in Earth's atmosphere was formed entirely by plants and microscopic blue-green algae (cyanobacteria).

Water and ice

◗ **Water is commonly found** as a solid, a liquid and a gas.

◗ **A compound** of the elements hydrogen and oxygen, water has the chemical formula H_2O.

◗ **Frozen water**, called water ice, floats because water is the only known substance less dense (heavy) as a solid than as a liquid.

◗ **However 'ice' may refer to** other frozen substances in very cold places, such as methane ice on Pluto and ammonia ice on Charon.

◗ **Water is fundamental** (basic) to all life on Earth. Between 55 and 70 percent of the human body is made up of water.

◗ **Earth is the only planet** in the Solar System to have liquid water on its surface.

◗ **Neptune has a deep ocean** of ionized water beneath its atmosphere of helium and hydrogen.

> **DID YOU KNOW?**
> Earth's oceans cover more than two thirds of the entire planet.

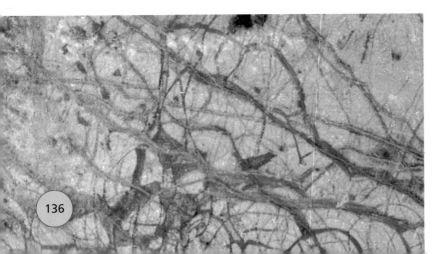

◄ *Jupiter's moon, Europa, may have oceans of water beneath its icy surface, and it is a major target in the search for life in the Solar System.*

- **Dried-up riverbeds** show that Mars once had surface water. There is ice at both poles and probably underground too.

- **Recently several spacecraft have discovered** signs of ice (frozen water) on the Moon.

▼ *A satellite view of Iceland, which shows the land covered in snow and ice.*

Mercury

🪐 **The nearest planet to the Sun** is Mercury. During its orbit, it is between 46.0 and 69.8 million km away. It has no moons.

🪐 **Mercury has the fastest orbit** – one journey around the Sun takes just 88 Earth days. Its average orbital speed is 47 km/sec.

🪐 **Twice during its orbit**, Mercury gets very close to the Sun and speeds up so much that the Sun seems to go backwards in the sky.

🪐 **Mercury rotates once every 58.6 Earth days**, but the time between one sunrise and the next is 176 Earth days, longer than Mercury's year.

🪐 **Temperatures change** from –190°C at night to more than 430°C (hot enough to melt lead) during the day.

🪐 **The crust and mantle** are made largely of rock, but the core (75 percent of its diameter) is solid iron.

🪐 **Mercury's dusty surface** is pocketed by craters made by space debris crashing into it.

🪐 **With less than six percent of Earth's mass**, Mercury is so small that its gravity can only hold on to a very thin atmosphere.

▼ *The Sun looks huge as it rises over Mercury. The sunny side of the planet is boiling hot, but the night side is more than twice as cold as Antarctica.*

Mercury is so small that its core has cooled and become solid (unlike Earth's). As this happened, Mercury shrank and its surface wrinkled.

Craters on Mercury discovered by the USA's Mariner 10 space probe have names such as Bach, Beethoven, Wagner, Shakespeare and Tolstoy.

▼ Mercury is a planet of yellow dust, as deeply dented with craters as the Moon. There is water ice in its deep polar craters, where the Sun never shines.

The Caloris Basin is a vast shallow crater, surrounded by mountains 2 km high

A thin crust of rock floats on top of the mantle

Mercury's huge iron core takes up three quarters of the planet

A layer of rock, called the mantle, surrounds the core

Mercury's surface is wrinkled by long, low ridges that probably formed as the planet's core cooled and shrank

139

Exploring Mercury

🪐 **Two spacecraft** have journeyed to Mercury and both returned high-quality information about this smallest of the planets.

🪐 **Mercury is by no means** the farthest planet from Earth, but it is difficult to get to. This is because it is so near the Sun that spacecraft have to counteract the Sun's immense gravity – which uses more fuel than leaving the whole Solar System.

🪐 **After a flyby** (close visit) of Venus, the US craft Mariner 10 arrived at Mercury in 1974.

🪐 **Mariner 10** took up a very long, lop-sided orbit that allowed three close approaches to Mercury, the last and nearest at 328 km above the surface.

🪐 **The craft mapped about half of Mercury's surface** and discovered information about the planet's very thin atmosphere and weak magnetic field.

🪐 **The second Mercury mission** was MESSENGER (MErcury Surface, Space ENvironment, GEochemistry, and Ranging), which left Earth in 2004.

🪐 **MESSENGER** made three flybys of Mercury in 2008–2009 before going into orbit in 2011. It mapped the areas not seen by Mariner 10, then in 2013 began an extended part of the mission.

🪐 **These further studies** included Mercury's rocky make-up and the chemical elements present on its surface, and more details of its thin atmosphere, magnetic field, and the possible presence of ice.

🪐 **In 2015** MESSENGER finally ran out of fuel and crashed into the planet's surface.

🪐 **A future Mercury mission** is the European-Japanese BepiColombo, for further mapping and atmosphere analysis, due around 2018–2020.

▼ *MESSENGER carried seven scientific instruments and took more than 250,000 images of Mercury. These pictures were taken at different wavelengths of light by the Mercury Atmosphere and Surface Composition Spectrometer, MASCS.*

Venus

🪐 **The second planet from the Sun** is Venus. Its orbit makes it 107.5 million km away at its nearest and 109 million km away at its furthest.

🪐 **Venus shines like a star** in the night sky because its thick atmosphere reflects sunlight amazingly well. This planet is the brightest object in the sky, after the Sun and the Moon.

🪐 **Venus is called the Evening Star** because it can often be seen from Earth in the evening, just after sunset. However, it can also be seen before sunrise. It is visible at these times because it is quite close to the Sun.

🪐 **The atmosphere of Venus** is mostly carbon dioxide gas with thick clouds containing sulphuric acid, given out by the planet's volcanoes.

◀ The thick clouds of Venus are made of carbon dioxide gas and sulphuric acid. They reflect sunlight and make the planet shine like a star. None of its atmosphere is transparent like Earth's, which makes it very difficult to see what is happening on the planet's surface.

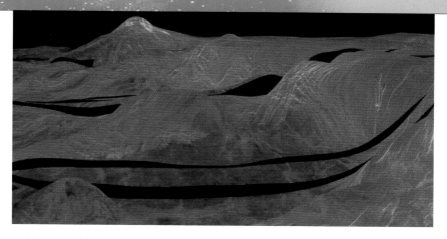

▲ *The 8-km-high volcano on the surface of Venus is called Maat Mons. Images have been created on computer using radar data collected by the Magellan orbiter, which reached Venus in the 1990s.*

Venus is the hottest planet in the Solar System, with a surface temperature of more than 460°C.

Venus is so hot because the carbon dioxide in its atmosphere traps the Sun's heat. This overheating is called a runaway greenhouse effect.

The thick clouds hide its surface so well that until the Russian Venera 9 probe landed on the planet in 1975, it was not known what was beneath the clouds.

Atmospheric pressure on the surface of Venus is 92 times greater than that on Earth.

A day on Venus (the time it takes to spin around once) lasts 243 Earth days – longer than its year, which lasts 224.7 Earth days. As Venus rotates backwards, the Sun comes up twice during the planet's yearly orbit – once every 116.8 Earth days.

Venus is the nearest planet to Earth in distance, as near as 38 million km, and in size, at 12,102 km in diameter.

Visitors to Venus

- **More than 40 craft** have been launched towards, flown close by, gone into orbit or landed on the surface of Venus, the closest planet to Earth.

- **After several US and USSR failures**, the first craft to reach another planet was the US's Mariner 2.

- **Mariner 2** flew past Venus in 1962 at a distance of 34,700 km and confirmed the planet had a thick cloud covering and was extremely hot.

- **In 1966** the USSR's Venera 3 became the first craft to reach the surface of another planet when it crash-landed.

- **In 1970** Venera 7 landed harder than it should have done, but still managed to send back the first radio signals from the surface of another planet.

- **Between 1989 and 1994** the US orbiting Magellan craft used radar (reflected radio signals) to 'see through' the thick clouds and map the spectacular mountains and valleys of almost the whole surface.

- **Europe's Venus Express** probe went into Venus orbit in 2006 and began an eight-year study of the atmosphere and surface.

- **Venus Express** made many discoveries, for example, lightning flashes are very common on the planet.

▼ *Venus Express was developed from the Mars Express mission and uses many similar parts. The main body of this space probe is very small compared to similar probes – just 1.8 m long and 1.4 m high.*

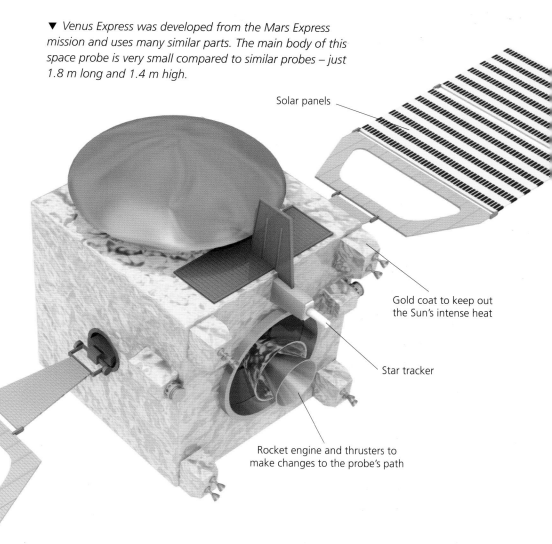

Solar panels

Gold coat to keep out the Sun's intense heat

Star tracker

Rocket engine and thrusters to make changes to the probe's path

🪐 **Venus Express** also detected a huge swirling area of gases at the South Pole.

🪐 **In addition,** Venus Express pointed its cameras and sensors towards Earth to try out ways of detecting signs of life – information that is now used when looking for life on other planets.

Earth

🪐 **The third planet from the Sun** is our home planet, Earth. Its average distance from the Sun is 149.6 million km, which is also 1 AU.

🪐 **The farthest point** of Earth's orbit from the Sun (aphelion) is 151.9 million km, and the nearest (perihelion) is 147.1 million km.

▼ *The inner core at Earth's centre is made of iron. It is very hot and keeps the outer core as a liquid. Outside this is the mantle, made of thick rock. The thin surface layer is called the crust.*

Crust

Mantle

Outer core

Inner core

- **Earth is the fifth largest planet** in the Solar System, with a diameter of 12,756 km and a circumference of 40,075 km at the Equator.

- **Along with Mercury, Venus and Mars**, Earth is one of four rocky or terrestrial planets. It is made mostly of rock, with a core of iron and nickel.

- **No other planet in the Solar System** has liquid water on its surface, so Earth is uniquely suitable for life. However more than 70 percent of Earth's surface is underwater.

- **The atmosphere is mainly harmless nitrogen** and life-giving oxygen, and it is more than 100–200 km thick. This oxygen has been made and maintained by plants over billions of years.

- **A magnetic field**, stretching 60,000 km out into space, protects Earth from the Sun's radiation.

- **Like the other Solar System planets**, Earth formed about 4.56 billion years ago.

- **Earth's orbit** around the Sun is 940 million km in length and takes 365.242 days.

- **Although Earth is tilted** at an angle of 23.5 degrees, it orbits the Sun on a level plane – the plane of the ecliptic. This is like a giant tabletop on which all the planets move.

- **The Earth is made up** of the same basic materials as meteorites and the other rocky planets – mostly iron (35 percent), oxygen (28 percent), silicon (17 percent), magnesium (15 percent) and nickel (2.7 percent).

Earth's formation

- **The Solar System was created** when the gas cloud left over from a giant supernova explosion began to collapse in on itself and spin.

- **About 4.56 billion years ago**, only a vast, hot cloud of dust and gas circling a new star, the Sun, existed.

- **Earth probably began** when tiny pieces of space debris (called planetesimals) were pulled together by each other's gravity.

- **As Earth formed**, more space debris kept on smashing into it, adding new material. This debris included ice from the edges of the Solar System.

- **About 4.53 billion years ago**, a rock the size of Mars crashed into Earth. The debris joined together to form the Moon.

- **The collision that created** the Moon made Earth very hot. Radioactive decay heated Earth even more.

- **For a long time**, Earth's surface was a mass of erupting volcanoes.

- **Iron and nickel** melted and sank to form the core. Lighter materials, such as aluminium, oxygen and silicon, floated up and cooled to form the crust.

DID YOU KNOW?
Earth's rotational speed makes it bulge in the middle.

5 At first, Earth's surface was made up of one large piece of land, but is now split into seven continents

▶ *The fiery young Earth gradually cooled until water condensed out of its steamy atmosphere to form oceans.*

1 Cloud starts to spin

4 Volcanoes erupt, releasing gases, which help to form the atmosphere

3 Earth begins to cool and a hard shell forms

2 Dust gathers into balls of rock, which then form a small planet

149

Earth's atmosphere

🪐 **Earth's atmosphere** is a blanket of gases, which we call air, that extends from the planet's surface up to a height of about 10,000 km.

🪐 **Most of the air is concentrated** in the lowest part of the atmosphere. The air gets progressively thinner with increasing altitude. Above 7000 m, there is not enough oxygen for people to breathe.

🪐 **Near the surface**, our atmosphere consists of nitrogen (78 percent), oxygen (21 percent) and small amounts of argon, carbon dioxide and other gases, together with a variable amount of water vapour.

🪐 **The atmosphere is divided** into a series of layers that have different characteristics.

🪐 **The lowest level is the troposphere**, which extends up to about 10 km average (range 5–20 km) above sea level. Weather and human activity are largely restricted to the troposphere.

🪐 **The stratosphere extends** from 10 km to about 50 km in altitude. It contains the ozone layer that shields Earth's surface from the harmful ultraviolet (UV) radiation in sunlight.

🪐 **Above the stratosphere** are the mesosphere (50–85 km) and the thermosphere (85–500-plus km). Most meteors that are seen burn up in the mesosphere or the upper stratosphere.

🪐 **The uppermost level** of the atmosphere is called the exosphere and extends between 500 and 10,000 km above Earth's surface. According to internationally accepted definitions, this part of Earth's atmosphere is actually in space.

- **The ionosphere** is the region around a planet that contains atoms and molecules that have been ionized by strong X-rays and UV light.

- **Earth's ionosphere** extends from around 50 km above sea level out beyond the atmosphere to about 1000 km.

- **The ionosphere** is made of charged particles, or ions. It contains a series of distinct layers, such as the Heaviside layer, that are used to reflect radio signals around the planet.

▶ *The various layers of the atmosphere (not shown to scale) provide an insulating and protective bubble around Earth.*

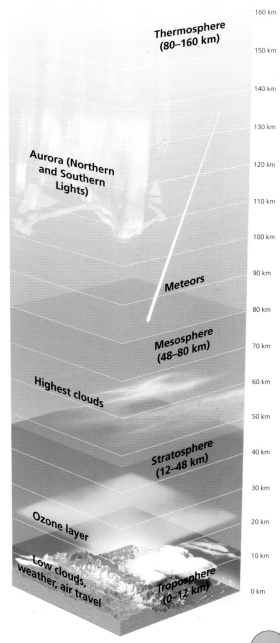

Thermosphere
(80–160 km)

Aurora (Northern and Southern Lights)

Meteors

Mesosphere
(48–80 km)

Highest clouds

Stratosphere
(12–48 km)

Ozone layer

Low clouds, weather, air travel

Troposphere
(0–12 km)

160 km
150 km
140 km
130 km
120 km
110 km
100 km
90 km
80 km
70 km
60 km
50 km
40 km
30 km
20 km
10 km
0 km

Magnetosphere

- **Earth's magnetosphere** is the region of space within the influence of Earth's magnetic field. The magnetosphere shields Earth from most of the effects of the solar wind.

- **Despite its name, the magnetosphere** is not spherical. Instead it is shaped like an elongated teardrop with the rounded end of the teardrop facing towards the Sun.

- **The sunward edge** of the magnetosphere is called the magnetopause and is located about 70,000 km from Earth.

- **Immediately to the sunward side** of the magnetopause is a shock wave (which is called the bow shock) caused by the solar wind being deflected by the magnetopause.

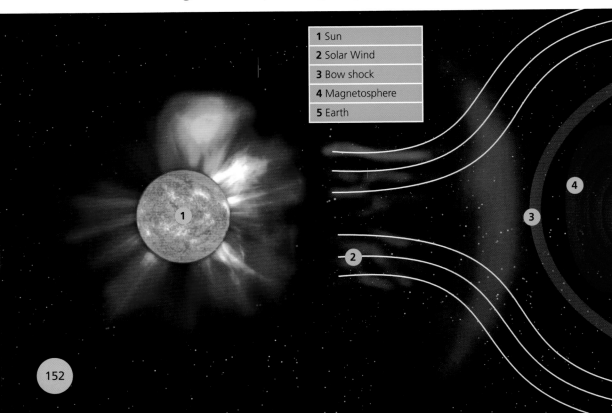

| 1 Sun |
| 2 Solar Wind |
| 3 Bow shock |
| 4 Magnetosphere |
| 5 Earth |

🪐 **On the side away from the Sun**, the magnetosphere trails away like the tail of a comet in what is known as the magnetotail.

🪐 **Although the magnetosphere deflects** most of the charged particles coming from the Sun and cosmic rays, some get through and become concentrated in two doughnut-shaped regions of radiation known as the Van Allen belts.

🪐 **Venus and Mars** are the only planets that do not have their own magnetosphere.

🪐 **Jupiter has by far the largest** magnetosphere and its magnetopause is located about 6 million km from the planet's surface.

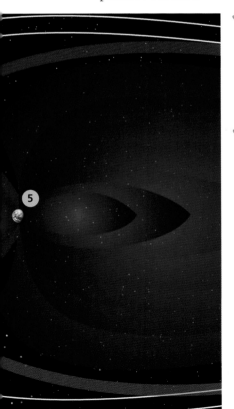

🪐 **The magnetism of Earth's Moon** is too weak to produce a magnetosphere, but two of Jupiter's moons, Io and Ganymede, have magnetic fields of sufficient strength.

🪐 **Stars also produce magnetic fields** and have magnetospheres. The Sun's magnetosphere is called the heliosphere and its magnetopause (called the heliopause) has a radius of more than 80 AU.

◄ *Earth's magnetosphere (shown in blue, with the bow shock in purple) is shaped by the constant pressure of the solar wind.*

Auroras

- **Bright displays of shimmering light** called auroras appear on some nights near the North and South Poles.

- **The aurora that appears** near the North Pole is the Aurora Borealis, also known as the Northern Lights.

- **The aurora that appears** near the South Pole is the Aurora Australis, or the Southern Lights.

- **Auroras are caused** by streams of charged particles from the Sun, known as solar wind, crashing into the gases of Earth's atmosphere.

- **Oxygen gas** glows a yellow-green colour when it is hit low in the atmosphere, and orange higher up.

- **Nitrogen gas glows bright red** when hit normally, and bright blue when ionized (electrically charged).

- **Haloes of light permanently exist** over each Pole, but they are usually too faint to see. They flare up brightly when extra bursts of energy reach Earth's atmosphere from the Sun.

- **Auroras only appear** at high latitudes, near the Poles, because there are deep gaps or cracks in Earth's magnetic field there.

- **When the solar wind** is blowing strongly, auroras are more spectacular.

- **New York in the US** and Edinburgh in the UK get an average of ten aurora displays every year.

◄ *The Northern Lights above the Arctic Circle look like curtains of bright colours.*

The Moon

🌀 **On average, the Moon is 384,400 km** from Earth and, at 3474 km across, it is just over 25 percent of Earth's diameter.

🌀 **Once every month**, the Moon orbits Earth. Each orbit takes 27.3 days. The Moon also spins around once on its axis in exactly the same time, so it keeps the same half facing Earth.

🌀 **The Moon is the brightest object** in the night sky, but like all planets and moons, it does not give out any light itself. It shines because its surface reflects sunlight.

🌀 **One half of the Moon** is lit by the Sun, but as it travels around the Earth, different amounts of this sunlit side are seen. This is why the Moon seems to change shape. These changes are called the phases of the Moon.

🌀 **A lunar month** is the time between one full Moon and the next. This is slightly longer than the time the Moon takes to orbit Earth because Earth is also moving.

🌀 **The Moon has almost no atmosphere** and its surface is simply dust, pitted with craters created by meteorites smashing into it early in its history.

New Moon — Waxing crescent Moon — First quarter Moon — Waxing gibbous Moon — Full Moon

▲ *During the first half of each monthly cycle, the Moon waxes (appears to grow) from a crescent-shaped new Moon to a full Moon. During the second half, it wanes (dwindles) back to a crescent-shaped old Moon.*

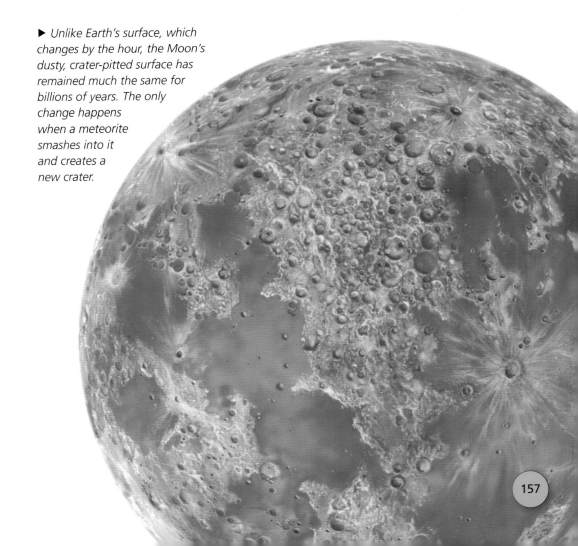

🪐 **On the Moon's surface** are large, dark patches referred to as seas because that is what people once believed they were. They are actually flat plains of hardened lava flows from ancient volcanoes.

🪐 **The side of the Moon** that is always turned away from Earth is called its far side, or, mistakenly, its 'dark' side – because during a new Moon phase this side is almost fully lit by sunlight.

▶ *Unlike Earth's surface, which changes by the hour, the Moon's dusty, crater-pitted surface has remained much the same for billions of years. The only change happens when a meteorite smashes into it and creates a new crater.*

157

Lunar features

Most of the craters on the Moon were formed during a period of many meteorite collisions, called the Late Heavy Bombardment, that began 4.1 billion years ago and ended 3.8 billion years ago.

This intense meteorite bombardment was followed by about 600 million years of volcanic activity when molten lava flooded out to cover the lunar seas. Since about 3.2 billion years ago, the Moon's surface has remained largely unchanged.

Tycho is the name given to the newest large crater. It was formed only about 110–105 million years ago, and has a diameter of 84 km.

▼ *Photographs from orbiting spacecraft reveal clear evidence of the numerous violent impacts that have shaped the Moon's surface features.*

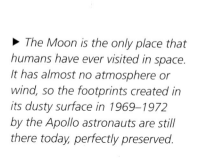

▶ *The Moon is the only place that humans have ever visited in space. It has almost no atmosphere or wind, so the footprints created in its dusty surface in 1969–1972 by the Apollo astronauts are still there today, perfectly preserved.*

🪐 **One of the most prominent craters** is Copernicus, which is a fine example of a ray-crater – it is surrounded by rays of pale material that were ejected from the crater by a meteorite impact.

🪐 **Aside from areas of bare rock**, most of the Moon's surface is covered by regolith – a mixture of dust and rock fragments that have been pulverized by meteorite impacts.

🪐 **Much of the rock** on the Moon is of a type called breccia and is composed of broken rock fragments that have been cemented together by lava.

🪐 **Astronauts have collected** nearly 400 kg of Moon rocks and brought them back to Earth for analysis and study.

🪐 **The most unusual** type of Moon rock is known as KREEP because it is rich in potassium (K), rare earth elements (REE) and phosphorous (P).

🪐 **In 2008 India's Chandrayaan-1 spacecraft** confirmed that water ice (frozen water) is present on the Moon.

🪐 **The next year NASA's** LCROSS mission released a small impactor that crashed into a shadowy polar area. The craft detected water from ice melted and thrown up by the impact.

Eclipses

🪐 **When one space object**, such as the Moon, blocks out the light from another, such as the Sun, an eclipse occurs.

🪐 **A lunar eclipse** is when the Moon travels behind Earth, and into Earth's shadow (Earth is between the Moon and the Sun).

🪐 **Lunar eclipses happen** about once or twice a year and last only a few hours.

🪐 **In a total lunar eclipse**, the Moon turns rust-red.

🪐 **Lunar eclipses can be seen** from anywhere on the half of Earth facing the Moon.

🪐 **A solar eclipse** is when the Moon comes between Earth and the Sun, casting a shadow up to 270 km wide on to Earth's surface.

Sun

▶ *This solar eclipse in Kenya shows the 'diamond ring' effect, when only one small area of sunlight passes the edge of the Moon, due to its uneven surface, and reaches Earth.*

In a total eclipse of the Sun, the Moon passes directly in front of the Sun, completely covering it so that only its corona can be seen.

There are at least two solar eclipses every year, but they are only visible from a narrow strip of the world.

Totality is when the Moon blocks out the face of the Sun completely. It only lasts for a few minutes.

Solar eclipses are possible because the Moon is 400 times smaller than the Sun, and is also 400 times closer to Earth. This means the Sun and the Moon appear to be much the same size in the sky.

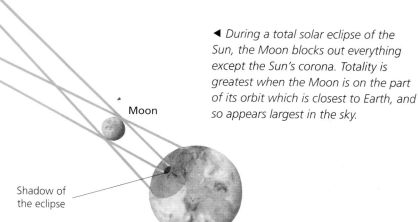

Moon

◀ *During a total solar eclipse of the Sun, the Moon blocks out everything except the Sun's corona. Totality is greatest when the Moon is on the part of its orbit which is closest to Earth, and so appears largest in the sky.*

Shadow of the eclipse

Earth

161

Moon probes

🪐 **The former USSR** (Russia and Soviet nations) scored several firsts and successes with its Luna programme.

🪐 **These included** the first spacecraft to pass near another space object, Luna 1, and the first to impact another space body, Luna 2, both in 1959.

🪐 **In 1966** Luna 9 was the first spacecraft to soft-land successfully on another space body.

🪐 **In 1969** the US Apollo missions were the first manned craft to orbit the Moon, then make the first landing with *Apollo 11*.

🪐 **Since those early missions** the US, Russia, Europe, Japan, China and India have all launched further moon probes.

🪐 **India's Chandrayaan-1** orbited the Moon from 2008 to 2009 and released a Moon Impact Probe that hit the surface; the soil and dust thrown up were analyzed for substances such as water ice.

🪐 **The US Lunar Reconnaissance Orbiter** (LRO) went into Moon orbit in 2009 to map the surface in great detail.

🪐 **Later that year** LRO's Lunar Crater Observation and Sensing Satellite (LCROSS) impactor smashed into the deeply shadowed crater Cabeus. This impact threw up debris that showed there was water ice on the Moon.

🪐 **As part of the X Prize collection**, the Google Lunar X Prize offers US$20 million for landing a robot rover on the Moon that can send signals and pictures back to Earth.

▲ *A replica of Luna 9, which landed in 1966. It was a sphere about one metre across that opened protective 'petals' to take photographs and measurements.*

Mars

⚬ **The nearest planet to Earth** after Venus is Mars. It has a daytime temperature and atmosphere more like Earth's than any other planet.

⚬ **Surface temperatures on Mars** range from −140°C in the winter polar regions at night to more than 30°C at the sunny summer equator by day.

⚬ **Mars is called the 'Red Planet'** because it is rust-red in colour. This comes from oxidized (rusted) iron in its soil.

⚬ **The fourth planet out from the Sun**, Mars orbits at an average distance of 227.9 million km. It takes 687 Earth days to complete its orbit – one Martian year.

⚬ **Mars is 6752 km in diameter** and spins around once every 24.62 Earth hours. This is almost the same amount of time that Earth takes to rotate once.

⚬ **Olympus Mons**, Mars' volcano is the biggest in the Solar System. It covers the same area as the UK and is three times higher than Mount Everest.

⚬ **The surface of Mars** is dry, rocky and covered in dust. The wind blows up huge dust storms, sometimes covering the whole planet. Dust devils, similar to small tornadoes, often race across the surface of Mars.

⚬ **Almost all the water on Mars** is frozen into ice. There are ice caps at the poles, and thin clouds made of ice crystals in the sky. Orbiting spacecraft have found ice hidden beneath the surface.

Apart from small amounts of ice crystals, the atmosphere of Mars is almost all carbon dioxide, with about two percent of the gas argon.

Mars was probably warmer and wetter in the past. Spacecraft have spotted many dried-up riverbeds, gullies and lake beds, and the Mars rovers, Spirit and Opportunity, have found minerals that normally form in water.

▶ Mars is the best known planet besides Earth. Studies have revealed a planet with a surface like a red, rocky desert – but there is also plenty of evidence that Mars was not always so desert-like.

Martian moons

- **Mars has two small moons**: Phobos, which is about 22 km in diameter, and Deimos which is only about 12 km across. They have so little gravity that an astronaut could leap off them and into space using muscle power alone.

- **Phobos means 'fear'** and Deimos means 'dread'. They are named after Greek mythological beings who accompanied their war god into battle.

- **American astronomer Asaph Hall** (1829–1907) discovered the Martian moons in 1877. Hall was director of the US Naval Observatory and later became Professor of Astronomy at Harvard.

- **Phobos and Deimos** are highly irregular in shape, commonly described as a 'lumpy potato'. They have every appearance of being asteroids that were formed when the Solar System was created and were subsequently captured by Mars' gravity.

- **Both moons follow** very low regular orbits around the planet. Deimos is at an average distance of about 23,500 km, while Phobos orbits just below 10,000 km above Mars' surface.

- **When viewed from the surface of Mars**, Phobos rises in the west and sets in the east twice each Martian day.

- **Large impact craters** caused by meteorites mark the surface of Phobos. The biggest, named Stickney, is 9 km in diameter and extends across almost one third of the moon's surface.

- **The meteorite craters** on Deimos have mostly been filled with dust and broken rock and none is more than 3 km across.

Due to its extremely low orbit, Phobos is being gradually slowed by Mars' gravity and is falling towards Mars' surface at a rate of 18 m per century. Phobos will crash into the surface of Mars in about 50 million years.

▼ *Phobos in close-up, showing the massive Stickney crater (at left) that dominates the moon's surface.*

167

Missions to Mars

🪐 **As the second-closest** planet to Earth, and one where life has the greatest chance of perhaps existing, Mars has been the target for more than 50 space missions.

🪐 **The former USSR** (Russia and allies) sent two rover missions to Mars in 1971 but both failed.

🪐 **In 1997** the US's Mars Pathfinder landed successfully and released the skateboard-sized rover Sojourner.

🪐 **In 2003** Europe's orbiting Mars Express released Beagle 2, a lander and crawler, but contact was lost.

🪐 **In 2015** images from the multi-purpose Mars Reconnaissance Orbiter showed that Beagle 2's solar panels had not unfolded away from its radio antenna.

🪐 **In 2003** the US sent two Mars rovers, Spirit and Opportunity. They travelled great distances and gathered much information, before Spirit ceased to work in 2010.

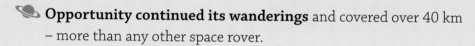

Opportunity continued its wanderings and covered over 40 km – more than any other space rover.

In 2012 the US's car-sized Curiosity rover arrived as part of the Mars Science Laboratory mission.

▼ *Curiosity is 2.9 m long and 2.2 m tall. It travels up to 200 m each day, depending on rocks, dust and other features of the terrain, and how much information it is gathering.*

DID YOU KNOW?

Many Mars missions have failed for various reasons including going off course, crashing into the planet, engineering problems and using up fuel.

169

Asteroids

Lumps of rock that orbit the Sun are called asteroids. Some were also known as minor planets.

Most asteroids are in the Main Asteroid Belt or Main Belt, which lies between Mars and Jupiter. Some much more distant asteroids are made of ice and orbit the Sun beyond Neptune.

There are more than one million asteroids bigger than one kilometre across. More than 200 asteroids are more than 100 km across.

A few asteroids come near Earth. These are called Near Earth Objects (NEOs).

Asteroids were once known as minor planets. New discoveries are recorded by the Minor Planet Center in Cambridge, Massachusetts, USA, which gives each one a unique catalogue number in addition to any name.

▼ Epsilon Eridani, a planetary system with two asteroid belts.

▶ *Impact by an asteroid estimated at 10–15 km across is suspected of wiping out the large dinosaurs and many other creatures and plants, in the mass extinction of 66 million years ago.*

In a reorganization of naming in 2006, the definition of the term asteroid was refined to exclude dwarf planets and certain other objects.

The first asteroid to be discovered was Ceres in 1801. It was detected by Giuseppi Piazzi, one of the Celestial Police, whose mission was to find a missing planet.

At 940 km across and 0.0002 percent of the Earth's mass, Ceres was the biggest asteroid. It is now classed as a dwarf planet.

DID YOU KNOW?
About every 50 million years, the Earth is hit by an asteroid measuring more than 10 km across.

Main Asteroid Belt

● **The Main Asteroid Belt is located** between the outermost rocky planet Mars and the innermost gas giant planet, Jupiter.

● **This is at a distance of 2.1–3.3 AU** from the Sun. The belt contains many thousands of objects, of which more than 100,000 have been individually identified.

● **Scientists believe that the Main Belt asteroids** are planetesimals left over from the formation of the Solar System. They were prevented from clumping together into a rock planet by the gravity of the massive gas planet Jupiter.

▼ *Shown here between Jupiter (left) and Mars (right), the Main Asteroid Belt forms a near perfect circle around the Sun.*

🪐 **Only one of the Main Belt asteroids**, Vesta, is bright enough to be seen with the unaided eye.

🪐 **Ida is one of the asteroids** photographed by the Galileo space probe. It has an irregular shape, 60 x 25 x 19 km. It was the first asteroid discovered to have its own natural satellite, called Dactyl.

🪐 **A tiny asteroid**, Dactyl measures just 1.5 by 1.2 km, and is egg-shaped. It orbits Ida at a distance of about 90 km.

🪐 **The original Jupiter Trojan asteroids** are located at the outer edge of the Main Belt in two groups. They follow the orbit of Jupiter at about the same speed but are at angles of 60 degrees to both Jupiter and the Sun. So they seem to chase Jupiter but do not get closer to the planet.

🪐 **The first Trojan** asteroid to be discovered was named Achilles in 1906. Many Trojan asteroids are named after warriors from the ancient Greek tales of the Trojan wars.

🪐 **The term Trojan** is now used for similar asteroid groups that have the same orbits as other planets, such as the Neptune Trojans and Mars Trojans.

🪐 **Other asteroids that orbit** in groups in the Main Belt are known as Hirayama families.

🪐 **These groups** are believed to be the remnants of larger asteroids that were smashed to pieces by collisions.

Visiting asteroids

🪐 **Asteroids, especially those** in the Main Asteroid Belt, have been visited by more than 30 probes including flybys, orbiters and landers.

🪐 **Some of these visits** have been flybys as part of longer missions. The first close-up photos of asteroids, Gaspra and Ida, were captured in 1991–1993 by the probe Galileo on its way to Jupiter.

🪐 **In 1996** the Near Earth Asteroid Rendezvous probe, NEAR-Shoemaker, set off to the 35-km-long asteroid Eros, which is a Mars-crosser, meaning it comes close to Earth within the orbit of Mars.

🪐 **On its way**, in 1997, NEAR-Shoemaker flew past the 50-km Main Belt asteroid Mathilde, sending back pictures that showed the lumpy potato appearance of most asteroids.

🪐 **NEAR-Shoemaker** went into close orbit of Eros in 2000 and landed there in 2001 – both firsts for asteroid exploration.

🪐 **The US craft Dawn** achieved another set of firsts following its launch in 2007.

🪐 **In 2011 in the Main Belt**, Dawn began to orbit Vesta, getting as close as 210 km to this huge 525-km asteroid.

🪐 **After being first** to visit Vesta, Dawn left in 2012 and in 2015 it was first to Ceres. At 950 km across, Ceres is the largest object in the Main Belt, and regarded as a dwarf planet.

🪐 **This meant that Dawn** thereby became the first spacecraft to orbit two space bodies.

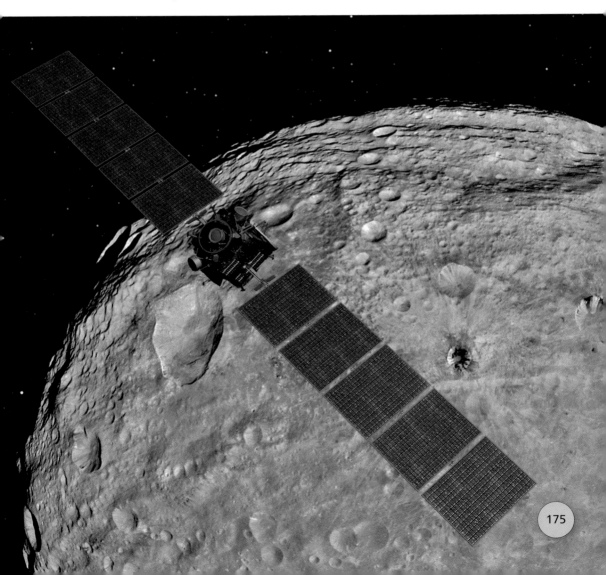

Japan's Hayabusa probe landed on the Mars-crosser asteroid Itokawa and after many problems managed to bring samples back to Earth in 2010.

▼ *Dawn orbited the huge asteroid Vesta at three different distances, the lowest being 210 km.*

175

Jupiter

🪐 **The biggest planet in the Solar System**, Jupiter is two-and-a-half times as heavy as all the other planets in our Solar System put together.

🪐 **Jupiter has no surface** for spacecraft to land on because it is made mostly of hydrogen and helium gas. The massive pull of Jupiter's gravity squeezes the hydrogen so hard that it is actually a liquid or even semi-solid at the planet's centre or core.

🪐 **Towards Jupiter's core**, immense pressure makes the liquid hydrogen behave like a metal.

🪐 **The ancient Greeks** originally named the planet Zeus after the king of their gods. Jupiter was the Roman name for Zeus.

🪐 **Jupiter spins around** in only 9.92 Earth hours, which means that its equator is moving at more than 45,000 km/h.

🪐 **It takes Jupiter 11.87 Earth years** to orbit the Sun, at an average speed of 46,800 km/h. Coupled with its very short day, this means one Jovian year lasts almost 10,500 Jovian days.

🪐 **The middle, or equator**, of Jupiter bulges out because the planet spins so fast. It churns up the planet's metal core and generates a magnetic field ten times stronger than Earth's.

🪐 **Jupiter has a Great Red Spot** – a huge swirl of red clouds, measuring more than 40,000 km across. The scientist Robert Hooke first noticed the spot in 1644.

🪐 **Jupiter is so big that the pressure** at its core makes it very hot. The planet gives out heat, but not enough to make it glow. If it were 70–100 times bigger, nuclear reactions would occur at its core and turn it into a star.

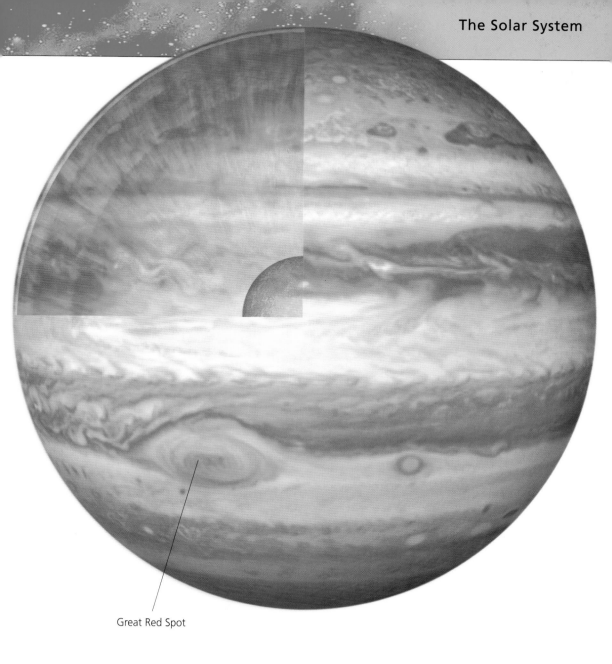

Great Red Spot

▲ *Jupiter is a gigantic planet, 142,984 km across at the equator. Its orbit varies between 740.9 and 815.7 million km from the Sun. The outermost layer is often pierced by huge lightning flashes, and temperatures here plunge to −150°C.*

Jovian moons

🪐 **The four biggest of Jupiter's 60-plus moons** are the Galilean moons. They were discovered in 1610 by Galileo, centuries before astronomers identified the other, smaller ones.

🪐 **Ganymede is the biggest** of the Galilean moons. At 5262 km across, it is larger than the planet Mercury.

🪐 **Ganymede looks solid**, but under its shell of ice is 900 km of slushy ice and water.

🪐 **At 4820 km across,** Callisto is the second biggest. It is scarred with craters from bombardments early in the Solar System's life.

🪐 **Io is the third biggest moon** at 3642 km across. Its surface is a mass of volcanoes caused by it being stretched and squeezed by Jupiter's massive gravity.

🪐 **The smallest Galilean moon** is Europa at 3121 km across. Its smooth icy surface is full of cracks, but beneath could be an ocean of water where there might be some forms of life.

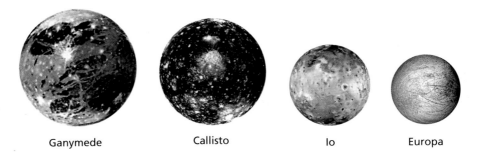

Ganymede   Callisto   Io   Europa

▲ *Galileo spotted Jupiter's four biggest moons in the 17th century. He used their orbits of Jupiter to argue against the geocentric theory that everything in the Universe went around Earth.*

Most of the other Jovian moons are less than 10 km across and were discovered by passing spacecraft. They orbit in groups, some at distances of more than 20 million km.

▼ *Io's yellow glow comes from sulphur, which is thrown out as far as 300 km by the moon's volcanoes.*

179

Jupiter flybys

🪐 **Eight spacecraft** have visited Jupiter. The first were Pioneer 10 and Pioneer 11 and Voyager 1 and Voyager 2, all in the 1970s.

🪐 **In 1992** the US-European Ulysses swung around Jupiter at a distance of 400,000 km on the probe's immensely lop-sided orbit.

🪐 **The opposite side** of Ulysses' orbit was close to the Sun, which was its main study target. The spacecraft did the same again in 2004 but at a distance of 120 million km.

🪐 **In 2000** the Cassini-Huygens mission whizzed past Jupiter, at a distance of 10 million km, on its way to Saturn.

🪐 **The Pluto-bound craft** New Horizons passed about 2 million km from Jupiter in 2007.

🪐 **The only probe** to orbit Jupiter was the US-German Galileo, which arrived in 1995 after a six-year voyage from Earth.

🪐 **On its way**, Galileo came close to the asteroids Gaspra and Ida.

🪐 **As it neared Jupiter** in 1994, Galileo observed comet Shoemaker-Levy 9 approach and break up as it encountered the gas giant.

🪐 **Nearer Jupiter**, in 1995, Galileo released a probe that plunged into the gas giant, sending back information for one hour before being crushed.

🪐 **From late 1995 Galileo's orbits** allowed it to make close studies of Jupiter and several inner moons including Io, Europa, Ganymede, Callisto and Amalthea.

🪐 **In 2003**, after eight years going around the giant planet, Galileo was deorbited and itself dived into Jupiter's vast clouds.

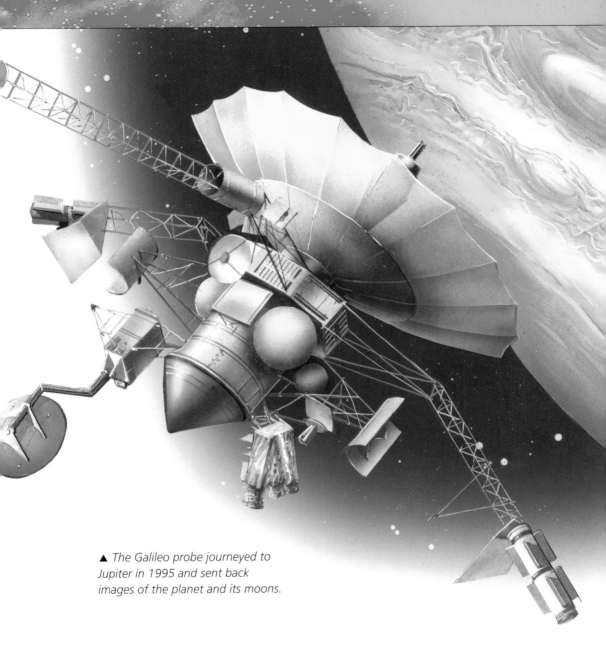

▲ The Galileo probe journeyed to
Jupiter in 1995 and sent back
images of the planet and its moons.

Saturn

- **The second biggest planet** in the Solar System is Saturn. It is 764 times as big in volume as Earth and measures an average of 116,465 km in diameter.

- **Saturn takes 29.5 Earth years** to travel around the Sun – that is, Saturn's year is 29.5 Earth years.

DID YOU KNOW?

Saturn's density is so low that it would float in water.

- **The planet's average distance from the Sun** is 1.43 billion km and its complete orbit is a journey of more than 4.5 billion km, at an average speed of 34,900 km/h.

- **Winds ten times stronger** than a hurricane on Earth swirl around Saturn's equator, reaching speeds of up to 1800 km/h.

- **Saturn is named after Saturnus**, the ancient Roman god of harvest. He was celebrated in the Roman festival of Saturnalia.

- **Saturn is made up of gases and liquids**, almost entirely hydrogen and helium. Only in the planet's very small core is there any solid material.

- **Since Saturn is so big**, the pressure deep inside is enough to turn hydrogen gas into a liquid. Further down, extreme pressure makes the liquid hydrogen act like a metal.

- **The surface of Saturn appears** smooth because the clouds are hidden under a layer of haze. However, the Cassini probe spotted lightning storms and a huge swirling storm near the pole.

🪐 **Saturn is one** of the fastest-spinning planets. Despite its size, it rotates in just 10.55 Earth hours. This means that its middle, or equator, moves at over 35,000 km/h.

🪐 **Like Jupiter**, Saturn's fast rotation makes it bulge at the equator. This means its diameter here is 120,540 km, while the diameter from pole to pole is 108,720 km – smaller by almost the width of the Earth.

Saturn's rings are made of many millions of tiny, ice-coated rock fragments

▲ *Saturn is almost as big as Jupiter, and made largely of liquid hydrogen and helium. It has a smooth surface (clouds of ammonia) and a shimmering halo of rings.*

Moons of Saturn

- **Saturn has more** than 60 officially described moons, with more than 50 named.

- **Largest of these is Titan**, which is the second biggest moon in the whole Solar System at 5150 km across – half as much again as Earth's Moon.

- **Titan is the sixth** closest of the main moons to Saturn, and makes up more than 19/20ths of the mass of all Saturn's moons.

- **Closest of the main moons** to the planet is Mimas, discovered in 1789 by William Herschel (1738–1822).

- **Mimas measures 398 km across** and orbits 186,000 km from its planet.

- **The gravity and orbit of Mimas** has helped to create a gap called the Cassini Division between Saturn's A and B rings.

- **In 2010 the Cassini probe** passed within 10,000 km of Mimas.

- **Most distant** of the main moons from Saturn is Iapetus.

- **Iapetus is 1470 km across**, 3.5 million km away and takes 79 Earth days to make one orbit.

- **Saturn has many more 'moonlets'**, some less than one kilometre across, that have not yet been formally described.

- **In terms of size**, some of these moonlets overlap with the largest chunks of rock and ice in Saturn's rings, although the moonlets orbit separately from the rings.

▼ *This view of Saturn shows the nearest of its main moons, Mimas, in the foreground. The huge crater on the near side, more than 130 km across with a ringed wall 6 km high, is named Herschel after the moon's discoverer.*

Saturn's rings

The rings of Saturn are chunks of water ice (frozen water), dust and tiny rocks that orbit the planet around its equator.

When sunlight hits the ice, the rings seem to shimmer as some parts reflect the light while others are in shadow.

▼ *The icy chunks in Saturn's rings range in size from a marble to a truck, each circling the planet in its own orbit.*

The **rings may be fragments** of a moon that was torn apart by Saturn's gravity before it formed properly.

Galileo was the first to see Saturn's rings, in 1610. His view through his early telescope was blurred and he said that it was as if the planet had ears.

Christiaan Huygens first realized that these shapes were actually rings in 1659.

First described were the two main sets of rings, A and B.

The A and B rings are separated by a gap called the Cassini Division, first spotted by Giovanni Cassini in 1675.

A third large ring called the C or *crepe* ring was identified closer to the planet in 1850.

From the 1980s, space probes revealed many other rings and 10,000 or more ringlets, some just a few metres wide and thick.

The known rings and groups are (moving from the planet) D, C, B, Cassini Division, A, Roche Division, F, Janus–Epimetheus, G, Methone, Anthe, Pallene, E and Phoebe. The A ring has its own subdivisions called the Encke and Keeler Gaps.

The rings and divisions interact with the planet's shepherd moons.

DID YOU KNOW?
Saturn's main rings measure over 900,000 km across, but only 20–50 m in thickness.

Shepherd moons

Shepherd moons are small natural satellites that help to determine the shape and structure of the rings around giant gas planets. They guide and confine the rings' rocks and dust in the way shepherds use trained sheepdogs to control their sheep.

The gap in Saturn's ring known as the Encke Division is swept clear of ring material by the planet's smallest and second-innermost moon, Pan, which was not discovered until images from Voyager 2 were re-examined in 1990.

The large shepherd moons Janus and Epimetheus help to define and maintain the neat outer edge of Saturn's D ring.

The shepherd moon Prometheus orbits on the inner edge of Saturn's F ring. It also interacts with other moons and its unusual orbit contributes to the F ring's braided appearance.

The Voyager 2 mission discovered a two-moon arrangement around Uranus. Two shepherd moons, Cordelia and Ophelia, maintain the inner and outer edges of the planet's Epsilon ring.

Four of Jupiter's inner moons – Metis, Adrastea, Amalthea and Thebe – are believed to affect the shape of this planet's faint ring system, which consists mainly of tiny dust particles.

Scientists believe that Jupiter's bright main ring is largely composed of material thrown up from the surfaces of Adrastea and Metis by meteorite impacts.

Jupiter's hazy second-outermost ring is often called the Amalthea Gossamer ring and is thought to be composed of fine dust from the surface of this moon.

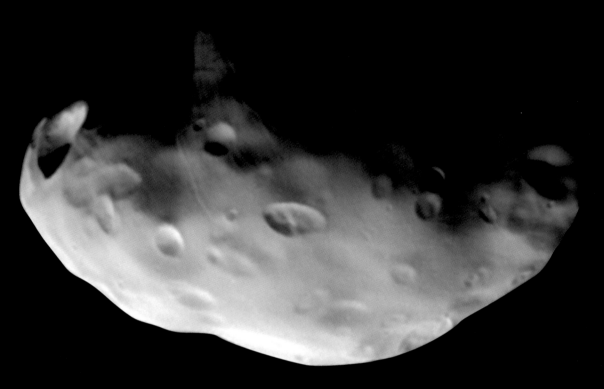

▲ *The interactions of shepherd and non-shepherd moons are complex. Saturn's Irregularly shaped, 105-km-long Pandora may help to shape or 'shepherd' the F ring's outer edge, but the combinations of local gravitational effects are unclear.*

Around Neptune, Despina – which is 180 km long – acts as the inner shepherd moon for the planet's Le Verrier ring, while 215-km-long Larissa may be a partial shepherd on the outer edge of the more prominent Adams ring.

The edges of Neptune's Adams ring are also marked by pronounced 'wiggles' that astronomers believe are caused by the gravitational influence of the moon Galatea.

Studying Saturn

- **Like other gas giants**, Saturn was visited by the long-distance US probes Pioneer 11 and Voyagers 1 and 2, in 1979, 1980 and 1981.

- **Each of these missions** discovered more moons and more features of the gas giant's ring systems.

- **The only other probe** to visit Saturn is Cassini-Huygens. It is regarded as one of the most successful outer Solar System missions. The huge craft, weighing more than 5 tonnes at lift-off (half being fuel), arrived in Saturn orbit in 2004. It had already flown past the moon Phoebe.

- **The orbits** of Cassini-Huygens also took it near Saturn's huge moon Titan, for close-up images and to gather other information.

- **In 2005** the craft separated, with Cassini staying in orbit, while the 320-kg lander Huygens, just 2.7 m across, approached Titan. For three hours Huygens descended through Titan's atmosphere on a parachute, sending information all the time.

- **After a slightly bumpy landing**, Huygens continued to send signals about the moon's surface for another 90 minutes.

- **Cassini then continued to study Saturn**, its moons and its rings, and make numerous discoveries about them all. Its radio signals take between 60 and 90 minutes to reach Earth.

- **Cassini's mission** has been extended several times and the orbiter is expected to remain active until 2018 and perhaps even 2020.

▲ Cassini-Huygens prepares to enter orbit around Saturn, in this artist's view. Huygens is the gold dish-shaped part in the right foreground. The grey bowl-shaped main antenna to the left is almost 4 m across.

191

Uranus

🪐 **Uranus is the seventh planet** out from the Sun. Its orbit keeps it 2870 million km away on average and takes 84 Earth years to complete.

🪐 **It tilts so far on its side** that Uranus seems to roll around the Sun. The angle of its tilt is 98 degrees, so its equator runs vertically. This tilt may be the result of a collision with a meteor or another planet many years ago.

🪐 **In summer on Uranus**, the Sun does not set for 20 Earth years. In winter, darkness lasts for over 20 Earth years. In autumn, the Sun rises and sets every nine Earth hours.

▶ The third largest planet in the Solar System, and with a faint ring system, Uranus is 51,118 km across its equator and has a mass 14.54 times that of Earth. The planet spins around once every 17.24 Earth hours, and it is the only planet to lie on its side. As it orbits the Sun, first one pole, then the equator, and then the other pole, faces the Sun.

🪐 **Uranus has more than 25 moons**, all named after characters from William Shakespeare's plays. There are five large moons – Ariel, Umbriel, Titania, Oberon and Miranda. Ten smaller moons were discovered by the Voyager 2 probe in 1986 and several more have been found since.

🪐 **Since Uranus is so far from the Sun**, it is very cold, with surface temperatures dropping to –225°C. Sunlight takes just eight minutes to reach Earth, but 2.5 hours to reach Uranus.

🪐 **Uranus' icy atmosphere** is made of hydrogen and helium. Winds circulate the planet at more than 600 km/h – six times as fast as hurricanes on Earth.

🪐 **The surface of Uranus** is not solid. Green-blue methane clouds surround the planet in an atmosphere of hydrogen and helium gas. Inside Uranus is an icy mixture of water, ammonia and methane, and probably a small, rocky core.

🪐 **Uranus is only faintly visible** from Earth with the naked eye, it looks like a very faint star, and was not identified until 1781.

🪐 **Uranus was named** after the ancient Greek god of the sky.

▶ *Uranus' moon Miranda looks as though it has been blasted apart, then put back together again.*

193

Neptune

🪐 **The eighth and outermost planet from the Sun** is Neptune. Its distance from Earth varies from 4459 million km to 4537 million km.

🪐 **Neptune was discovered in 1846**. Two mathematicians, Englishman John Couch Adams (1819–1892) and Frenchman Urbain Le Verrier (1811–1877), told astronomers where to look after they worked out where a new planet should be from the effect of its gravity on Uranus.

🪐 **Neptune is so far from the Sun** that its orbit lasts 164.8 Earth years. It has only completed slightly more than one orbit since it was discovered in 1846.

🪐 **Like Uranus**, Neptune is shrouded in blue methane clouds at temperatures as low as –220°C in a deep atmosphere made of hydrogen and helium gas.

🪐 **Unlike Uranus**, which is almost plain blue all over, Neptune has white clouds, created by heat inside the planet.

🪐 **Neptune has the strongest winds** in the Solar System, blowing at up to 2000 km/h.

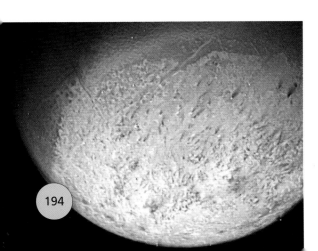

◄ *Neptune's moon Triton is green, while its icecaps of frozen nitrogen are pink. It also has volcanoes that erupt fountains of ice. It is one of the coldest places in the Solar System with a surface temperature that goes below –220°C.*

Great Dark Spot

▲ *Neptune is the fourth largest planet. At 49,528 km across, it is slightly smaller than Uranus, but it is actually a little heavier. Like Uranus, its clouds of incredibly cold methane make it blue in colour, and it has a thin ring system. However Neptune's poles are at right angles to the Sun and the ecliptic, so it does not orbit 'on its side' like Uranus.*

🪐 **The eight largest moons** of Neptune are named after characters from Greek myths. More than five additional small moons have been discovered, one as recently as 2013.

🪐 **The Great Dark Spot** was a giant storm seen by Voyager 2 in 1989. It then disappeared but other huge spots form and fade.

195

Visiting the outer gas giants

🪐 **The outer gas giants** have each been encountered only once, Uranus in 1986 and Neptune in 1989.

🪐 **Amazingly**, it was the same craft that made each flyby – the long-travelled US probe Voyager, which had left Earth in 1977.

🪐 **Voyager 2** passed about 82,000 km from Uranus and sent back what are still the only close-up images of the planet.

🪐 **The craft** discovered two new rings, 10 new moons, and that Uranus has a magnetic field similar in strength to Earth's.

🪐 **Voyager 2** also took photographs and measurements of some Uranian moons including Puck, Miranda, Titania, Ariel, Umbriel and Oberon.

DID YOU KNOW?

When Voyager 2 encountered Neptune, it was so far away that its radio signals took more than four hours to reach Earth.

● **After leaving Uranus**, Voyager 2 headed to the outermost Solar System planet, Neptune, a journey that took three and a half years.

● **The close encounter** took Voyager 2 to about 4500 km from Neptune's cloud tops.

● **Before this flyby**, the craft passed the Neptunian moon Nereid at a distance of 4.7 million km.

● **Five hours after the Neptune flyby**, Voyager 2 passed within 40,000 km of Triton, Neptune's largest moon.

● **Voyager 2 discovered** six new moons, more rings, details of the cloud movements, and an accurate measurement of the length of the Neptunian day (the time taken for the planet to rotate once).

▼ *This artist's view of Uranus is from Ariel, its second nearest moon. Ariel is 1155 km across and orbits 191,000 km from the planet, and has many ridges, craters, mountains, valleys and other features.*

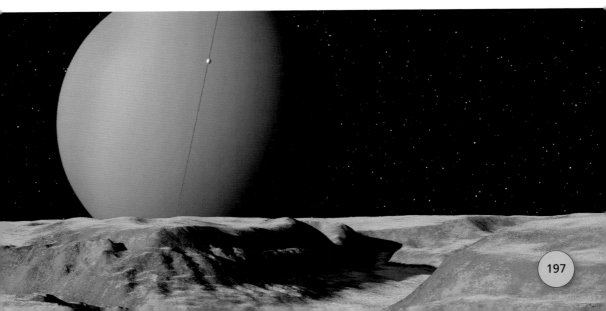

Kuiper Belt

Beyond the outermost planet, Neptune, is a region of the Solar System called the Kuiper Belt.

Thought to be shaped like a fairly flattened doughnut, the Kuiper Belt is named after Dutch-born US astronomer Gerard Kuiper (1905–1973).

Neptune's distance from the Sun is about 30 AU.

The Kuiper Belt extends from 30 AU to perhaps 50–55 AU from the Sun.

Objects in the Kuiper Belt and beyond are called TNOs, trans-Neptunian objects, because they are beyond Neptune's orbit.

The Kuiper Belt itself is home to a subgroup of TNOs called KBOs, Kuiper Belt objects. They include dwarf or minor planets such as Pluto and Eris.

▲ *Artist impressions of the Kuiper Belt (and Main Asteroid Belt) often show bodies close together for effect. In reality there are immense distances between them.*

There are also smaller objects that resemble asteroids, composed mainly of various forms of ice, such as frozen ammonia and methane.

Despite being home to probably more than 100,000 KBOs over 100 km across, the total mass of the Kuiper Belt is far less than Earth's mass.

The outer edge of the Kuiper Belt overlaps with the next farthest region of the Solar System, the Scattered Disc.

The Scattered Disc then blurs into the Solar System's immense and outermost region, the Oort Cloud.

199

Dwarf planets

🪐 **From about 2000**, the discovery of more Pluto-like bodies orbiting the Sun led to astronomers to rethink the definition of the term planet. The term minor planet includes objects that are not planets or comets.

🪐 **One subcategory** of minor planets is asteroids, including those in the Main Asteroid Belt, and Trojan asteroids.

🪐 **Another subcategory** is dwarf planets. These are large enough for their gravity to cause them to form into a spherical or ball shape, but not massive enough to dominate other objects.

🪐 **The first discovered dwarf planet** in 1801 was Ceres, previously called an asteroid, in the Main Belt.

🪐 **Next was Pluto**, back in 1930.

🪐 **Sedna**, named after the Inuit goddess of the sea, was found in 2003 and may be a dwarf planet.

🪐 **Dwarf planet Haumea** was identified in 2004 and named in 2008. It is about as far from the Sun as Pluto and 1900 km across.

🪐 **Next came Eris**, in 2005. It is very slightly smaller than Pluto, at around 2325 km across.

◄ *This artist's view of dwarf planet Eris shows its tiny moon Dysnomia, probably between 300 and 400 km across, in the foreground.*

▲ *Before receiving its official name, Eris – Greek goddess of turmoil – was nicknamed Xena. It takes 559 years to orbit the Sun.*

However Eris is 25–30 percent heavier than Pluto, making it the most massive dwarf planet.

At its farthest, Eris's elongated orbit is twice the distance of Pluto's, in the region called the Scattered Disc.

Makemake was also found in 2005. It orbits the Sun at a similar distance to Pluto, and is 1500 km in diameter.

Pluto

When it was discovered in 1930 by US astronomer Clyde Tombaugh (1906–1997), Pluto became the ninth planet – but it was by far the smallest at 2372 km across.

- **Since 2006**, Pluto has been reclassified as a dwarf planet by the International Astronomical Union, IAU.

- **Pluto has a tilted and elongated** orbit that varies from 4437 million km to 7310 million km from the Sun, which is almost 50 times farther out than Earth.

- **This enormous distance** means Pluto is mostly in the region beyond Neptune, called the Kuiper Belt.

- **At this distance**, Pluto takes 248 years to travel once around the Sun, even at its average speed of 16,800 km/h. For 20 years of this time, Pluto is closer than Neptune to the Sun.

- **It spins around in 6.4 Earth days**, so its day lasts nearly as long as an Earth week.

- **It is mainly a mix of rock** and frozen substances such as nitrogen, methane and ammonia. Nitrogen ice covers most of Pluto's surface.

- **The very thin atmosphere** contains gases of nitrogen, methane and carbon monoxide.

- **Pluto has five moons**, the first of which was discovered in 1978.

- **Much about Pluto** remained a mystery until it was visited by the New Horizons spacecraft in 2015.

◄ *Pluto as imaged by New Horizons in 2015. The massive craterless 'Heart' feature lower right is officially named Tombaugh Regio.*

Moons of Pluto

- **In 1978**, US astronomer James Christy (1938–) discovered that Pluto had a large moon, which was named Charon.

- **Charon is by far the largest moon** in the Solar System compared to its planet – about 1208 km across, which is half Pluto's width, and one ninth of its mass.

- **Charon orbits Pluto** at an average distance of almost 19,600 km.

- **Like Pluto**, Charon is probably a mix of rock and various kinds of ice, with a mostly ice-covered surface.

- **In 2005**, two tiny moons were discovered orbiting Pluto. They are named Nix and Hydra.

- **Nix is only 54 km long** and orbits about 48,700 km from Pluto.

- **Hydra is the outermost of the moons**, at 64,700 km from Pluto. It is 43 km long.

- **Kerberos** was discovered in 2011. It is just 14 km across and its average orbital distance is 57,800 km.

- **Discovered in 2012**, Styx is the smallest moon, with a length of only 7 km. It is the second most distant from Pluto after Charon, at 42,600 km.

▼ *Charon endures temperatures as low as –260°C in winter, rising to a 'warm' –212°C in summer. This is a realistic or natural-colour photograph from New Horizons.*

205

Encounter with Pluto

⚪ **In 2015** NASA's New Horizons craft reached Pluto after an immense journey that lasted nine and a half years.

⚪ **This was the farthest** distance any spacecraft had travelled – a distance of 4700 million km from Earth.

⚪ **About the size** of a grand piano, and weighing almost half a tonne when launched, New Horizons has a 2.1-m dish to send and receive radio signals.

⚪ **As they were so far away**, the radio signals from New Horizons took about four and a half hours to reach Earth.

⚪ **New Horizons first went past Jupiter** in 2007 at a distance of 2.3 million km, to gain a gravity-assist – or slingshot – for extra speed.

⚪ **After entering** the Kuiper Belt in July 2015, the craft flew within 12,500 km of Pluto itself, at a speed of almost 14 km/sec.

⚪ **New Horizons took thousands** of pictures and sensor readings of the dwarf planet and its moons.

⚪ **Images showed** that Pluto was far more colourful and had many more surface features than expected.

⚪ **This suggests** its rocks and ice, far from being still and inert, are active and still evolving.

⚪ **One giant pale area** 1600 km across, nicknamed 'The Heart' due to its shape, has been named Tombaugh Regio, or Tombaugh's Region, after Pluto's discoverer.

⚪ **New Horizons** continued into deep space, and aims to fly past Kuiper Belt object 2014 MU69 in 2019.

▲ *New Horizons passes Pluto, with its relatively huge moon Charon beyond. At such a distance the Sun looks little more than an ordinary, although bright, star.*

Oort Cloud

🪐 **The Oort cloud is a bubble- or shell-like region** that marks the outermost reaches of the Solar System.

🪐 **The innermost part** of the Oort Cloud is perhaps 5000 AU from the Sun, or as close as 2000 AU.

🪐 **Earth's average** distance from the Sun is one AU, astronomical unit. The outermost part of the Oort Cloud is 50,000, perhaps 100,000 AU, or even farther from the Sun.

🪐 **The inner parts** of the cloud merge into the Scattered Disc, which itself overlaps on its inside with the Kuiper Belt at about 50 AU.

🪐 **The Oort Cloud** is thought to be home to perhaps trillions of long-period comets that loop around the Sun, then head back into the cloud's icy blackness.

🪐 **It probably formed** when the early Sun and planets came into being from a swirling disc, then the gravities of the outer gas giants, especially Jupiter, threw material far out into space.

🪐 **If the Oort Cloud** is as big as some estimates suggest, it stretches halfway to the nearest stars, Proxima and Alpha Centauri.

🪐 **The Oort Cloud** is named after Dutch astronomer Jan Oort (1900–1992).

🪐 **Jan Oort** made many advances in understanding the Solar System and the Milky Way galaxy, and suggested comets came from some vast, far-off area.

▶ *The top of this diagram shows (1) the Solar System, with the four inner planets, Main Asteroid Belt and Jupiter. In the stage below are the four outermost planets and the Kuiper Belt (2). Lastly, at the bottom we see their place in the Scattered Disc, with the Oort Cloud all around it (3).*

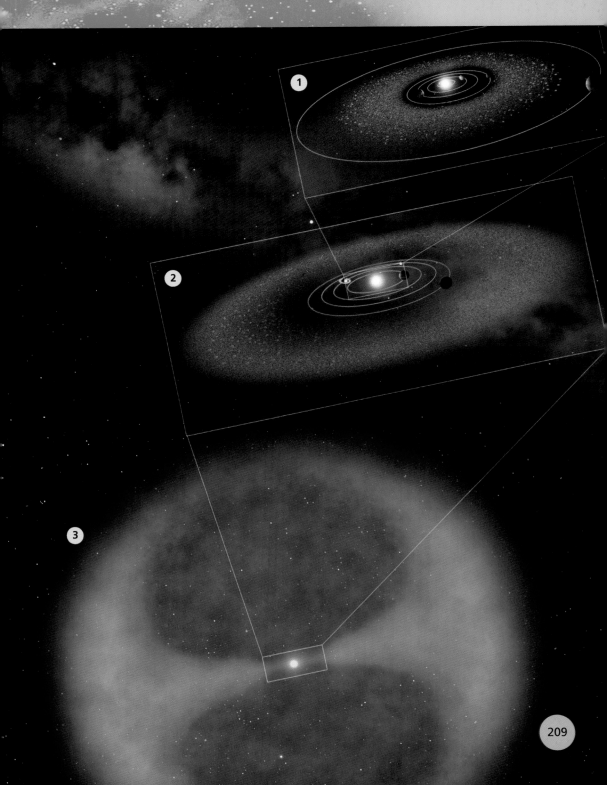

Comets

- **Bright objects with long tails**, comets can sometimes be seen glowing in the night sky – and bright ones even by day.

- **They may look spectacular**, but most comets are balls of ice, dust and rocky fragments, usually only a few kilometres in diameter.

- **Many comets orbit the Sun**, but their orbits are very long and they spend most of the time in the far reaches of the Solar System. They are seen when their orbits bring them close to the Sun for a few weeks.

- **A comet's tail forms** as it nears the Sun and its head, or nucleus, begins to warm up and outgas (eject gases, vapours and particles).

- **The tail is a vast plume** of gas millions of kilometres long, blown by the solar wind; it shines as sunlight catches it. There may also be a thin atmosphere or coma around the nucleus.

◄ Comets are often named after their discoverers, especially Australian astronomer Robert McNaught. He has found more than 80 comets and almost 500 asteroids, including the famously bright comet C2006/P1.

▲ *Comet West, which visited the Sun in 1976, was bright enough to see in daylight. Its white dust tail and blue gas tail do not trail behind but always point away from the Sun.*

Periodic comets appear at regular intervals. Short-period comets come from the Kuiper Belt and long-period ones come from the Oort Cloud.

Some comets reach speeds of 2 million km/h as they near the Sun. Far from the Sun, they slow down to about 1000 km/h.

Comet McNaught (C/2006 P1) in 2007 was the brightest for almost half a century. It was non-periodic, which means it is unlikely to be seen again, or at least, not for many centuries.

The Shoemaker-Levy 9 comet smashed into Jupiter in July 1994, with the biggest space impact ever witnessed, especially by the Galileo space probe. This was an unusual comet in that it orbited Jupiter, not the Sun. It had probably been captured by Jupiter's gravity a few decades earlier.

Halley's comet

🪐 **Halley's comet** is named after the British scientist and astronomer Edmund Halley (1656–1742).

🪐 **He forecast that the comet** would return in 1758, which was 16 years after his death. This was the first time a comet's arrival had been accurately predicted.

🪐 **Halley's comet orbits** the Sun every 75.3 years, on average.

🪐 **Its innermost orbit loops** between Mercury and Venus, and at its far point stretches out beyond Neptune.

🪐 **Chinese astronomers described** a visit of Halley's comet as long ago as 240 BC.

🪐 **When Halley's comet** was seen in AD 837, Chinese astronomers wrote that its head was as bright as Venus and that its tail stretched right across the sky.

🪐 **King Harold II of England** saw the comet in 1066. When he was defeated by William the Conqueror a few months later, people interpreted the comet's visit as an evil omen.

▼ *Halley's comet was embroidered on the Bayeux Tapestry, which shows Harold's defeat by William at the Battle of Hastings in 1066.*

DID YOU KNOW?

Halley's comet was seen in about 12 BC, so some say it was the Bible's Star of Bethlehem.

▲ Halley's comet came close to Earth in 1986. Its next visit will be in 2061.

Probing comets

- **The first spacecraft** to fly close past a comet was Europe's Giotto, in 1986.

- **Giotto approached within 600 km** of the head or nucleus of Halley's comet.

- **In fact Halley's comet** was the target for five space probes, called the Halley Armada. As well as Giotto it was observed by Vegas 1 and 2 (Russia–France) and Suisei and Sakigake (Japan).

▼ *This artist's impression shows Rosetta's Philae lander on the surface of comet 67P/Churyumov-Gerasimenko. In fact Philae set down at an angle on an uneven, well-shaded site.*

- **In 2004** the European mission Rosetta–Philae took off for comet 67P/Churyumov–Gerasimenko.

- **Rosetta–Philae** flew past Mars in 2007 at a distance of 250 km, then within 800 km of asteroid Steins in 2008, and 3160 km from asteroid Lutetia in 2010.

- **On arrival** at Churyumov–Gerasimenko in 2014, Rosetta–Philae went into orbit about 30 km from the comet, which measures about 4 km long and wide.

- **In November 2014** Rosetta released the small lander Philae, which is one metre across and weighs just 20 kg.

- **After 'bouncing' twice** off the comet, which has tiny gravity because it is so small, Philae came to rest on its surface – the first-ever landing on a comet.

- **Philae touched down in a shadowy area**, so its batteries were recharged only irregularly by its solar panels, meaning communications were erratic.

- **Philae ceased working in July 2015**, but it has sent much information about the comet's make-up back to Earth via orbiting Rosetta.

DID YOU KNOW?

The first 'bounce' of Philae took it more than one kilometre away from the comet before it returned.

Meteors

🪐 **Meteoroids are billions** of small rocks that hurtle around the Solar System. Most are no bigger than a pea but a few are several metres across.

🪐 **Most meteoroids that encounter Earth** are very small and burn up when they enter Earth's atmosphere.

🪐 **Streaks of light** seen in the night sky are these burning meteoroids leaving fiery trails, which are known as meteors.

🪐 **The streaks of light** are also called shooting stars, but they have nothing to do with stars.

🪐 **Meteor showers are bursts** of dozens or hundreds of burn-up trails or meteors, often occurring as Earth passes through a dust trail left by an earlier comet.

🪐 **Meteor showers** are named after the constellations they seem to come from, in a radiating pattern like fireworks.

🪐 **The heaviest showers** are the Quadrantids (3–4 January), the Perseids (12 August) and the Geminids (13 December).

🪐 **Meteorites are larger space rocks** that penetrate through Earth's atmosphere and reach the ground.

DID YOU KNOW?

Most meteorites encounter Earth's atmosphere at speeds of over 20 km/sec.

▶ *Most meteoroids that enter Earth's atmosphere burn up in the stratosphere to produce bright streaks of light, called meteors or shooting stars.*

Meteorites

🪐 **Meteorites are small** solid objects from space, called meteoroids, that have impacted with the surface of a planet or moon. They weigh less than 1000 tonnes.

🪐 **The largest known Earth meteorite** weighs some 60 tonnes, and is still lying where it fell at Hoba West in Namibia, Africa.

🪐 **Discovered in Greenland** by the explorer Robert Peary in 1897, the largest meteorite fragment on public display weighs 34 tonnes. Called Ahnighito ('Tent'), it is in the Hayden Planetarium in New York, USA.

🪐 **Meteorites found on Earth** can be divided into three main categories, popularly known as irons, stones and stony-irons.

🪐 **Irons, which used to be called siderites**, are composed almost entirely of the metals iron and nickel (or alloys of the two) and when found their outer surface is often covered with rust.

🪐 **Stones, which used to be called aerolites**, are composed of silicate minerals such as pyroxene, olivine and feldspar, together with a small amount of nickel or iron.

◀ When cut, polished and treated with acid, a nickel-iron meteorite reveals distinctive patterning that is named Widmanstatten, after the Austrian mineralogist who discovered the phenomenon in 1804.

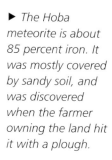

▶ *The Hoba meteorite is about 85 percent iron. It was mostly covered by sandy soil, and was discovered when the farmer owning the land hit it with a plough.*

🪐 **There are two sub-types** of stony meteorites – chondrites, which often have a rounded appearance and a structure made up of tiny rock spheres known as chondrules, and achondrites, which usually have a jagged appearance and do not contain chrondrules.

🪐 **Stony-irons**, which used to be called siderolites, are composed of silicate minerals and nickel-iron in roughly equal proportions.

🪐 **About 85 percent** of Earth meteorites are stony chondrites, 8 percent stony achondrites, 5 percent iron, and only 1–2 percent stony-iron.

🪐 **Tektites are small, rounded objects** made of silica glass. Previously thought to be meteorites, it is now accepted that tektites are produced by the impact of an asteroid striking Earth.

🪐 **Good places to find meteorites** are Antarctica and Western Australia because there has been so little human activity there.

Meteorite craters

🪐 **The most famous** and best-preserved crater on Earth is the Meteor Crater in Arizona, USA. It is incorrectly named, as it was made by a meteorite – not a meteor. It measures 1250 m in diameter and is 175 m deep.

🪐 **A nickle-iron meteorite** about 50 m in diameter and weighing about 300,000 tonnes formed Meteor Crater some 50,000 years ago. Most of the meteorite is still buried beneath the crater walls, although some fragments are on display in a local museum.

▼ *Meteor Crater, also known as the Barringer Crater, in Arizona has been well preserved in the dry conditions.*

Near Henbury in northern Australia is a group of 13 separate craters that must have been formed by the fragments of a meteorite which broke up moments before it impacted Earth.

Most meteorite craters on Earth's surface have been eroded almost out of existence, but geologists can still detect the telltale scars that are called as astroblemes (star wounds).

Small meteorite impacts cause distinctive horsetail-shaped features in rock that are known as shatter cones.

Measuring some 24 km across, the Ries basin in southern Germany was caused by a meteorite about one kilometre in diameter. The town of Nördlingen is built on the dried-up bed of a lake that once filled the crater.

The 100-km Manicouagan Crater in Canada is more than 200 million years old. A ring-shaped lake has formed around the 'peak' at the centre of this much-eroded crater.

Scientists have discovered the remains of the 180-km Chicxulub Crater beneath the sea floor and land on the coast of the Yucatàn Peninsula in the Gulf of Mexico. Now partly eroded and filled with seabed mud and other debris, it is likely that this crater was caused by the asteroid strike that may have wiped out the great dinosaurs and many other life forms, 66 million years ago.

Seabed drilling has revealed the existence of a crater 85 km in diameter beneath the waters of Chesapeake Bay on the east coast of the USA. The crater was identified by fragments of shocked quartz, which are only formed by meteorite impacts.

Astronomy

Astronomy

🪐 **The study of the night sky** is called astronomy – from the planets and moons to the stars and galaxies.

🪐 **Astronomy is one of the most ancient** of all the sciences, dating back at least 5000 years.

🪐 **The ancient Egyptians used their knowledge** of astronomy to work out their calendar and to align the pyramids.

🪐 **The word 'astronomy'** comes from the ancient Greek words *astro* meaning 'star', and *nomia* meaning 'law'.

🪐 **Since the early 1600s** astronomers have used telescopes to study objects that are too faint and small to be seen with the naked eye.

🪐 **Space objects give out** other kinds of radiation besides light, such as radio and ultraviolet waves. Astronomers have special equipment to detect these rays and waves.

🪐 **Professional astronomers today** usually study photographs and computer displays instead of staring through telescopes. This is because many space objects only show up on long-exposure photographs.

🪐 **Astronomers can spot new objects** in the night sky by laying a current photographic view over an old one and looking for differences.

🪐 **Professional astronomy involves** sophisticated equipment costing billions. Yet even 21st century amateurs make important

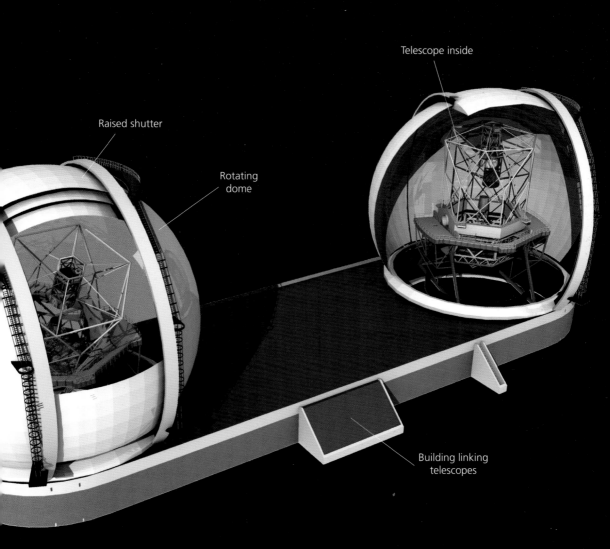

Telescope inside

Raised shutter

Rotating dome

Building linking telescopes

▲ *The two Keck telescopes at the Mauna Kea Observatories each have their own round dome with shutters that open to let in the starlight.*

The night sky

🪐 **When we look at the night sky** we can see the Moon and many twinkling points of light.

🪐 **Most lights in the sky** are stars. Moving, flashing lights may be aircraft, weather balloons or Earth-orbit satellites.

🪐 **Often the brightest 'stars'** in the night sky are not actually stars at all, but the planets, Jupiter, Venus and Mars.

🪐 **A total of 6000 stars** can be seen from Earth with the unaided or naked eye, with 2000 visible from any one place.

🪐 **The pale band across** the middle of the sky is a side-on view of our galaxy, the Milky Way.

🪐 **The pattern of stars** seems to rotate (turn) each night as Earth spins. It takes 23 hours and 56 minutes for the star pattern to return to the same place in the sky.

🪐 **As Earth orbits the Sun** each year, our view of the stars changes and the pattern starts in a different place each night.

🪐 **Different arrangements** of stars are seen in the Northern Hemisphere and the Southern Hemisphere.

🪐 **Over millennia**, the real positions of stars change since they are all moving through the Universe.

> **DID YOU KNOW?**
> The Andromeda Galaxy is over 2.4 million light years away, but can be seen clearly with the naked eye.

▲ *With the unaided eye, about 2000 stars can be seen twinkling in the night sky. Stars twinkle because of the shimmering of heat in the Earth's atmosphere. Some of these stars are trillions of kilometres away and their light takes thousands of years to reach us.*

Star patterns

🪐 **Seeing patterns** in the arrangement of stars in the sky is undoubtedly very ancient and predates civilization.

🪐 **The first evidence** of described and named constellations comes from Mesopotamia (modern Iraq) in about 3000 BC.

🪐 **The Mesopotamians named** some of their constellations after animals, for example 'the lion', and others after occupations, such as 'the herdsman'.

🪐 **Ancient Egyptians interpreted** the constellations as representing their gods and goddesses. The modern constellation Draco was the hippopotamus-headed goddess Tawaret, while Ursa Major was seen as a jackal, symbolizing the god Set.

🪐 **Ancient Chinese astronomers** arranged the night sky in an entirely different manner.

🪐 **They grouped the stars** into 28 lunar mansions that were then divided into four groups – the Red Bird of the south, the Black Tortoise of the north, the Blue Dragon of the east and the White Tiger of the west.

🪐 **The individual mansions** had names that were mostly taken from everyday life, such as the Encampment, the Roof, the Room, and the Winnowing-basket.

🪐 **In ancient India**, astronomers arranged the night sky into 27 divisions that were known as nakshatras. Each nakshatra was centred on a particular star or planet and was associated with a certain god or goddess.

In Australia, under clear desert skies, the Aborigines interpreted the night sky as pictures and patterns in the areas of relative darkness between the stars.

Easily identifiable patterns of stars that do not form a whole constellation are called asterisms. The most famous asterism is the Big Dipper (which in Britain is known as the Plough) that forms part of Ursa Major.

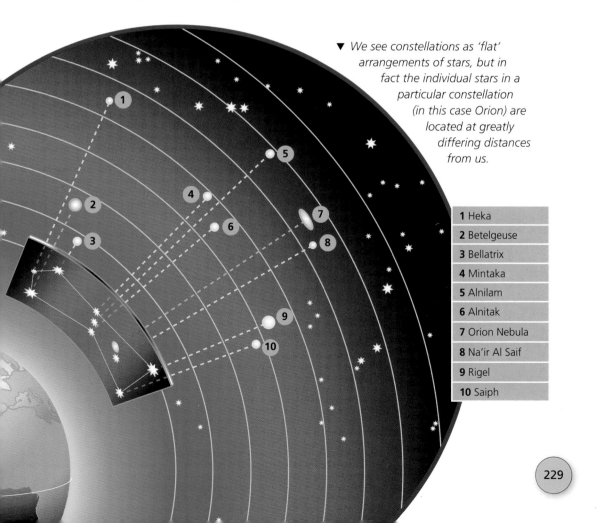

▼ We see constellations as 'flat' arrangements of stars, but in fact the individual stars in a particular constellation (in this case Orion) are located at greatly differing distances from us.

1	Heka
2	Betelgeuse
3	Bellatrix
4	Mintaka
5	Alnilam
6	Alnitak
7	Orion Nebula
8	Na'ir Al Saif
9	Rigel
10	Saiph

Zodiac

- **The zodiac is the band of constellations** that the Sun appears to pass in front of during the year as the Earth orbits the Sun. It lies along the ecliptic.

- **The ecliptic is the plane** of Earth's orbit around the Sun. The Moon and all the other planets lie in this plane.

- **The ancient Greeks divided** the zodiac into 12 parts, named after the constellation they saw in each part. These are the signs of the zodiac.

- **The 12 constellations of the zodiac** are Capricorn, Aquarius, Pisces, Aries, Taurus, Gemini, Cancer, Leo, Virgo, Libra, Scorpio and Sagittarius.

- **Astrology (which is different from astronomy)** holds that the movements of the planets and stars in the zodiac affect events and shape people's lives.

- **For astrologers**, all the constellations of the zodiac are equal in size.

- **However the Earth has tilted** slightly since ancient times and the constellations no longer correspond to the zodiac. So the dates that the Sun seems to pass in front of each constellation no longer match the dates astrologers use.

- **However the Moon and planets** stay within the band of the zodiac as they move across the sky.

▼ *The zodiac signs are imaginary symbols that ancient astronomers linked to star patterns.*

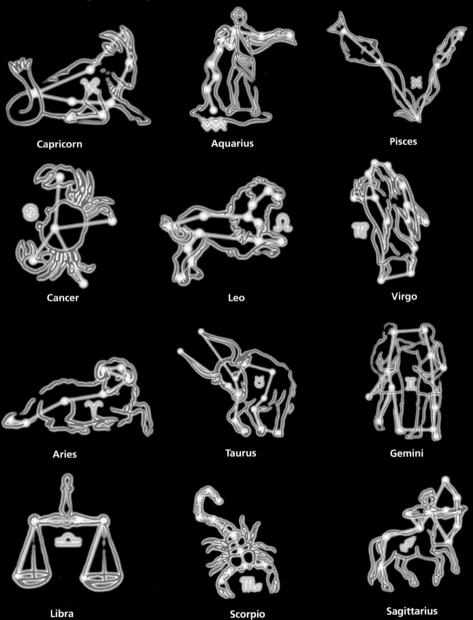

Capricorn

Aquarius

Pisces

Cancer

Leo

Virgo

Aries

Taurus

Gemini

Libra

Scorpio

Sagittarius

231

The Milky Way

🪐 **On clear, dark nights**, the Milky Way can be seen as a pale glowing band that stretches right across the sky.

🪐 **The Milky Way is actually the galaxy** that Earth, the Sun and Solar System are inside.

▼ *The Milky Way seems to whirl across the sky but this effect is caused by Earth's rotation. Most of the stars and galaxies orbit its centre at speeds of hundreds of kilometres per second.*

- **The Romans were the first** to use the phrase Milky Way (*Via Lactea*). The ancient Greek astronomers called it the Milky Circle (*Kiklos Galaxias*).

- **According to Greek myth**, the goddess Hera produced the milk in the Milky Circle to feed the infant hero Hercules.

- **Some Native American peoples** regarded the Milky Way as the route taken by ghosts on their way to the afterlife.

- **The Inuit peoples of Alaska** and northern Canada saw the Milky Way as a pathway of glowing ashes that led weary travellers home.

- **For Aborigines**, the patches of darkness in the Milky Way made a picture of a giant emu stretching across the heavens.

- **In the 7th century**, Korean astronomers marked the position of stars with black dots on white paper and they showed the Milky Way as a thick black band.

- **Galileo was the first astronomer** to observe the Milky Way through a telescope and discover its true nature as 'congeries of innumerable stars'.

- **German philosopher Emmanuel Kant** (1724–1804) was first to speculate that if the Milky Way was a galaxy of stars, then there might be other, more distant, 'Milky Ways' visible in the night sky.

- **The astronomer William Herschel** was the first to draw a map of what the Milky Way might look like if viewed from the outside. His disc-shaped image became known as the grindstone model.

- **By studying** the distribution of globular clusters in the Milky Way, the American astronomer Harlow Shapely (1885–1972) was able to deduce that the Sun was located near the edge of the Milky Way.

Space catalogues

 **Since ancient times** astronomers have made lists, charts and other records of stars in the night sky.

 **We now know that some of those light sources** are not stars but other objects, so they have their own kinds of non-stellar (non-star) lists and catalogues.

 **Some of those objects are planets**, and some are comets.

 **Others are galaxies** (vast groups of stars) or nebulae (massive clouds of dust).

 **The first modern catalogue** of non-stellar objects was made by astronomer Charles Messier (1730–1817).

 **One of the main modern lists** of non-stellar objects is the New General Catalogue of nebulae and star clusters (NGC).

 **The advent of radio astronomy** brought a whole new area of catalogues for objects that give out no or little light, but which emit many other kinds of similar electromagnetic energy, such as radio waves, microwaves and X-rays.

 **Radio sources** are listed in some of these catalogues, such as Cambridge University's 3C catalogue.

 **For example**, the first quasar to be discovered was listed as 3C 273. Quasars are immense sources of light, radio and other waves and energy.

▶ *With such an immense number of stars, galaxies and nebulae in the night sky, astronomers need detailed catalogues to locate each kind of object reliably and check whether it has already been identified and investigated.*

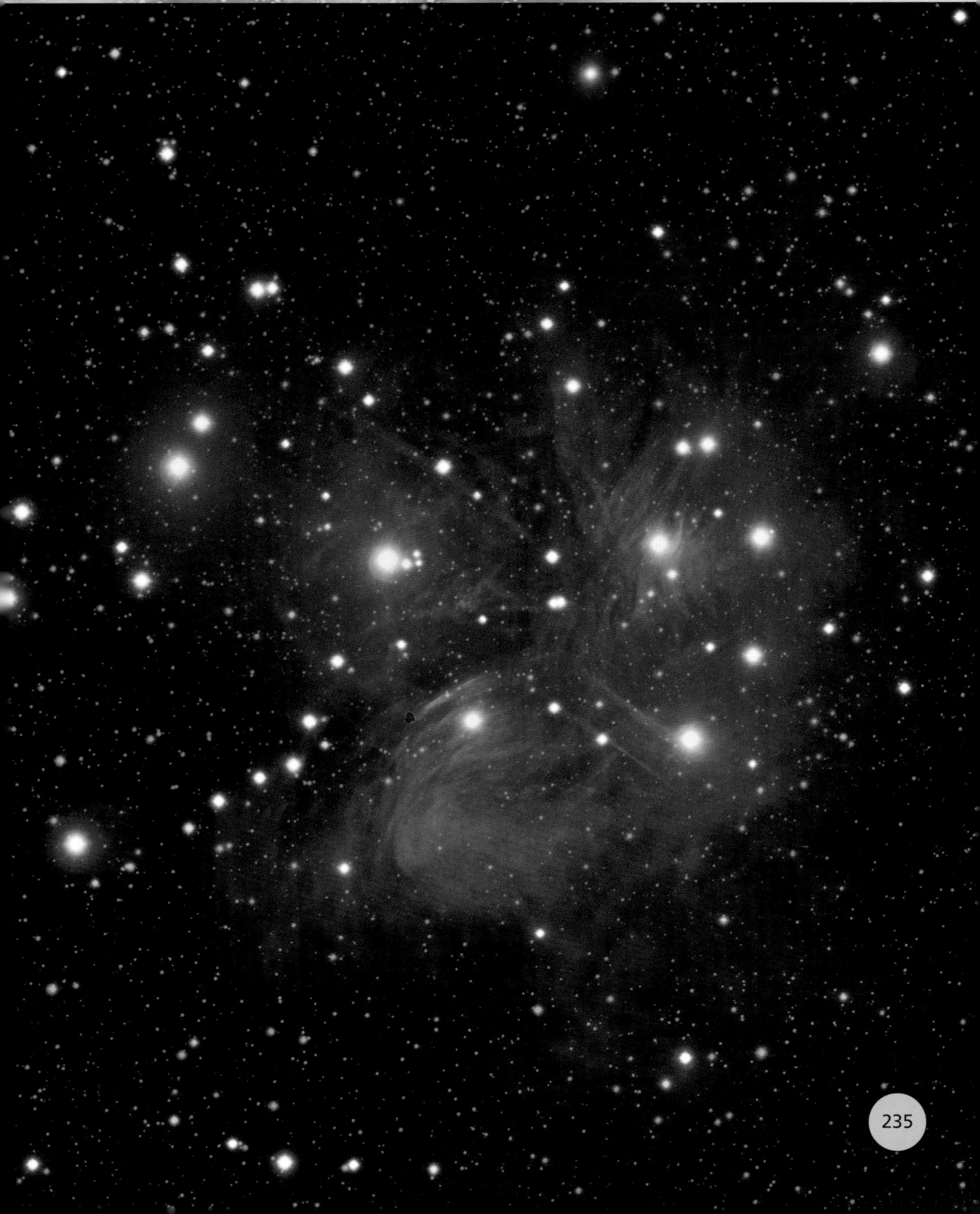

Telescopes

🪐 **Optical telescopes** magnify distant objects using lenses or mirrors to focus light rays, which makes an enlarged image of the object.

🪐 **Other telescopes detect** radio waves, X-rays or other kinds of electromagnetic radiation.

🪐 **Refracting telescopes** are optical telescopes that use lenses to refract (bend) the light rays.

🪐 **Reflecting telescopes** are optical telescopes that focus light rays by reflecting them off curved, dish-like mirrors. They make the light rays turn back on themselves so they are shorter than refracting telescopes.

🪐 **Most professional astronomers** do not gaze at the stars directly. Their telescopes record light using electronic sensors called Charge-Coupled Devices (CCDs), as in digital cameras and smartphone cameras. The astronomers can then look at the results on screen later.

🪐 **Most early discoveries** in astronomy were made with refractors.

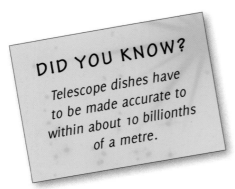

DID YOU KNOW?

Telescope dishes have to be made accurate to within about 10 billionths of a metre.

Platform for direct observation

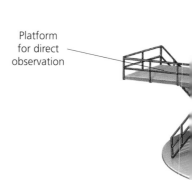

● **Modern observatories** use gigantic reflector dishes made up of hexagons of glass or coated metal.

● **Large telescope dishes** are continually monitored and tweaked by computers to make sure that the reflector's mirrored surface stays completely smooth.

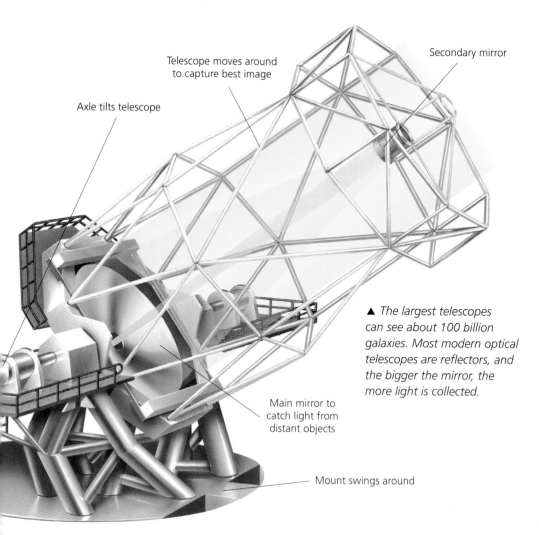

Telescope moves around to capture best image

Secondary mirror

Axle tilts telescope

▲ The largest telescopes can see about 100 billion galaxies. Most modern optical telescopes are reflectors, and the bigger the mirror, the more light is collected.

Main mirror to catch light from distant objects

Mount swings around

237

Amateur astronomy

🪐 **Around the world**, many people are involved in astronomy as amateurs – in their spare time as a hobby or interest – rather than as a job or profession.

🪐 **There are probably** more than 100 million amateur astronomers worldwide, as well as people who take an occasional interest to watch, for example, an eclipse or meteor shower.

🪐 **Britain has more than 200** official astronomy societies and groups, based in towns, cities, counties and country areas.

🪐 **The world's largest database** for star brightness is coordinated by the AAVSO, American Association of Variable Star Observers. It has records of more than 20 million observations.

🪐 **Amateur astronomers** have also discovered hundreds of notable comets through the years, as well as thousands of minor comets and other objects.

🪐 **Most active amateur astronomers** have their own home telescopes and many also use larger telescopes at their local club or society.

🪐 **Since the 1990s** computers have led to more sophisticated equipment such as the semi-automatic GoTo telescope set-up.

🪐 **A GoTo telescope** is moved by motors and its field of view is analyzed by computer.

▶ *A keen part-time astronomer sets up and aims cameras ready to record both short- and long-exposure images. These pictures may be sent to a central database for comparison to pick out any new objects.*

If the name of a target object is keyed in, the telescope can 'go to' or point at it and show it on screen – even if the telescope is outside and the observer is warm indoors.

Gran Telescopio Canarias

🪐 **The Gran Telescopio Canarias** (GTC) or Great Canary Telescope is a large optical (light-receiving) telescope of the reflecting design.

🪐 **It is sited** at the Roque de los Muchachos Observatory, 2300 m above sea level on the island of La Palma.

🪐 **La Palma** is part of the Canary Isles, which are part of Spain, in the Atlantic Ocean off north-west Africa.

🪐 **The lack of pollution**, air clarity, low artificial light levels, ocean position, fine weather and general atmospheric conditions of La Palma make it one of the best places in the Northern Hemisphere for astronomical studies.

🪐 **The GTC has a single aperture** (opening) with a main or primary curved mirror that has an effective or working size of 10.4 m – the largest in the world.

▼ *The great cost of modern telescopes, at more than £100 million for the GTC and £8 million per year to run, means location is all important to ensure maximum cloud-free, clear views.*

▲ *The GTC's array of mirrors is visible at the bottom of the main cage within the observatory. The metal frame is built from special alloys so it does not shrink or expand with changing temperature.*

The mirror is actually made of 36 hexagonal (six-sided) units working together.

The telescope's planning began in 1987, and it was built between 2001 and 2008.

The GTC's first light – the first time it detected a proper view – was in 2007.

The main nation operating the GTC is Spain, along with contributions from Mexico's National Autonomous University and the USA's University of Florida.

As well as the GTC, the Roque de los Muchachos Observatory is home to more than a dozen telescopes and similar astronomical devices.

Keck telescopes

🪐 **The twin Keck** optical telescopes are sited on Mauna Kea, Hawaii – one of the world's best places for astronomy.

🪐 **The Keck telescopes** are the main devices at the W M Keck Observatory, founded by and named after petroleum tycoon William Myron Keck (1880–1964).

🪐 **The Keck Foundation** donated more than $140 million to establish the W M Keck Observatory and its twin Keck telescopes.

🪐 **Building began** in 1985 and the Keck I telescope began observing in 1990. The construction of Keck II followed and it began its studies in 1996.

▼ *Mauna Kea is home to many telescopes. This view shows Keck I and II in the centre, with the Japan-operated Subaru Telescope to the left and NASA's Infrared Telescope on the right.*

🪐 **Each Keck telescope** has a reflecting design with a main curved mirror 10 m across.

🪐 **This main mirror** is actually made up of 36 hexagonal (six-sided) segments all functioning as one huge mirror.

🪐 **Each telescope** weighs about 300 tonnes and moves to point at various parts of the sky by electric motors and gears.

🪐 **Rather like how we see with two eyes**, the views from Keck I and Keck II are combined to give incredible detail and precision of light sources in the night sky.

🪐 **As well as detecting light**, the Keck telescopes pick up near infrared, that is, infrared waves which are only slightly longer than the red waves of the light spectrum.

🪐 **The Keck Observatory** is managed by a combination of US organizations including the University of California, California Institute of Technology, University of Hawaii, NASA and National Optical Astronomy Observatory.

Observatories

🪐 **Observatories are buildings** that house telescopes and other equipment, and from where astronomers study space as well as Earth's atmosphere and weather.

🪐 **For the best view** most observatories are on mountain tops, far from interference by artificial lights and above some of Earth's blurring atmosphere.

🪐 **In most observatories**, the telescopes are housed in a domed building, which turns around to aim anywhere in the sky.

🪐 **The oldest existing observatory** is thought to be a prehistoric circle built about 7000 years ago in Goseck, Germany.

🪐 **At the Beijing Ancient Observatory**, China, there are 500-year-old bronze astronomical instruments.

🪐 **The first British observatory** was the Royal Greenwich Observatory, London, founded in 1675.

▼ *The Kitt Peak National Observatory is near Tucson, Arizona, USA. It is 2095 m above sea level and houses 24 optical and two radio telescopes and many other kinds of equipment.*

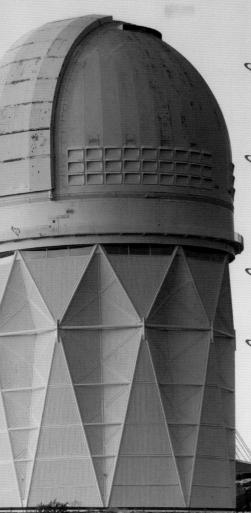

🪐 **The highest observatory** on Earth is 5640 m above sea level, at Cerro Chajnantor in the Atacama Desert of Chile.

🪐 **The lowest 'observatory'** is 1.7 km below sea level, in Homestake Mine, South Dakota, USA. Its 'telescope' is actually tanks of heavy water that trap neutrinos from the Sun.

🪐 **The first photographs** of the stars were taken in 1840 on the then newly invented photographic film.

🪐 **Today, most observatories** rely on sensitive electronic cameras, photographs and computers rather than the eyes of astronomers.

245

Mauna Kea

🪐 **Mauna Kea** is a dormant (currently inactive) volcanic mountain on the main 'Big Island' of Hawaii, which is in the mid Pacific Ocean and a state of the USA.

🪐 **Mauna Kea** is home to several astronomy and space centres known as the Mauna Kea Observatories.

🪐 **The observatories** are sited here because of the excellent seeing conditions – they are located at a height of 4200 m above sea level, which is above much of the local weather.

🪐 **Mauna Kea** also has low pollution and light levels, a generally clear climate and calm atmospheric conditions for much of the year. However the threat of earthquakes and violent storms (such as hurricanes or typhoons) means that great precautions must be taken to protect the telescopes.

🪐 **There are about 12 main** telescope arrays on Mauna Kea, including the twin Keck telescopes.

🪐 **Most of these telescopes work** with visible light and/or infrared rays.

🪐 **One of the largest** is Japan's Subaru Telescope, from a Japanese term meaning unite, which began working in 1998.

🪐 **The Subaru Telescope** has the reflecting design with a main mirror 8.2 m across.

🪐 **This main mirror** is one single structure, called monolithic, rather than being composed of many smaller parts, known as segmented.

The Canada-France-Hawaii Telescope (CFHT) has a mirror 3.6 m across. As well as the three nations in its name, it is used by organizations in China, Taiwan, Korea and Brazil.

▼ *On Mauna Kea in the foreground is the Gemini North Telescope, GNT. It works with its counterpart, GST (South) in Chile, South America. Together they see almost all of the skies visible from Earth.*

Southern observatories

🪐 **As well as observatories** in North America, Europe and Asia, there are many astronomy and space centres in the Southern Hemisphere.

▼ *These South African Astronomical Observatory (SAAO) telescope domes house reflecting telescopes with mirrors 1.9 m, 1 m, 0.75 m and 0.5 m across. Silvered blinds reduce the heat taken in during the day to protect the very delicate structures and equipment inside.*

🪐 **These include the Paranal Observatory**, more than 2600 m above sea level in the Atacama Desert, northern Chile, South America.

🪐 **The Paranal Observatory** has clear skies almost every night as well as almost no local artificial light or pollution. The very dry air also means very low levels of water vapour of humidity, which can cause observing problems.

🪐 **One of the main telescopes** at Paranal is the Very Large Telescope, VLT.

🪐 **Also in Chile** is the southern part of the Gemini Observatory, situated 2700 m up in the Andes Mountains. The northern part of the Gemini Observatory is on Mauna Kea.

🪐 **Each of these observatories** has a Gemini reflecting optical telescope with a main mirror 8.2 m across.

🪐 **The two telescopes** are networked to cover an enormous area of the night sky.

🪐 **Australia has Siding Spring Observatory**, which is 1160 m high, and is situated near Coonabarabran, in central-north New South Wales, Australia.

🪐 **Siding Spring** has more than 20 working telescopes including the optical reflecting Anglo-Australian Telescope (AAT), which has a main mirror 3.9 m across.

🪐 **The huge SALT telescope** is located at the South African Astronomical Observatory (SAAO), the national observatory of that country, near Sutherland in the south-west.

Spectra and emission lines

🪐 **Light from the Sun**, stars and other sources can be studied using an instrument called a spectrograph, which is attached to the viewing end of a telescope.

🪐 **The spectrograph has a very small**, slit-like aperture at the telescope's point of focus so that only the light from a particular source enters the instrument.

🪐 **Inside the spectrograph**, a device called a collimator turns the cone of light into parallel rays. These are then split into a rainbow-like spectrum by a prism of glass or similar transparent material.

🪐 **A spectrum with more blue than red** indicates a very hot star, such as a white dwarf, while a spectrum with more red than blue indicates a large, fairly cool star such as a red giant.

🪐 **Each of the chemical elements** absorbs and emits light at very precise wavelengths and these produce spectral lines that can be used to identify the different elements present in a star.

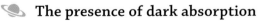

🪐 **The presence of dark absorption lines** superimposed on a continuous spectrum shows that some of the light has been absorbed on its way to Earth. For example, carbon absorption lines may indicate that the light has passed through a cloud of interstellar dust.

DID YOU KNOW?
A continuous spectrum of colours is produced by the hot, dense surface of a star such as the Sun.

▲ *At Kitt Peak, Arizona, the McMath–Pierce Solar Telescope has a moveable 3-m mirror to send sunlight down a 152-m shaft. Its two spectrographs to study the Sun's light are about half way down.*

🪐 **Clouds of high-temperature**, low-pressure gas, such as nebulae, produce a spectrum that consists only of a series of bright emission lines.

🪐 **Wide emission lines indicate** a rapidly rotating or expanding gas that may have been produced by a supernova (exploding star).

🪐 **Astronomers also study spectra** at wavelengths other than that of visible light. In radio astronomy, the 21-cm-long hydrogen line is particularly important because hydrogen is by far the most abundant element in the Universe.

251

Radio telescopes

🪐 **Radio telescopes are used** to pick up radio waves and other similar kinds of waves, made of electromagnetic energy, instead of light waves.

🪐 **The first radio telescope** was built by Karl Jansky in New Jersey, USA in 1932. It looked like a long wire strung on scaffolding.

🪐 **Most modern radio telescopes**, like optical reflecting telescopes, have a big dish to collect and focus data.

🪐 **At the centre of its dish**, a radio telescope has an antenna (aerial or receiver) to pick up radio signals.

🪐 **Radio waves are much longer** than light waves, so radio telescope dishes are very big, up to 100 m or more across.

🪐 **Instead of one big dish**, some radio telescopes use a collection of small, linked dishes. The further apart the dishes are, the sharper the image.

🪐 **Radio galaxies are very distant** and only faintly visible (if at all), but they can be detected because they give out radio waves.

🪐 **Radio astronomy** led to the discovery of pulsars and background radiation from the Big Bang.

🪐 **Radio astronomy proved** that the Milky Way is a disc-shaped galaxy with spiralling arms.

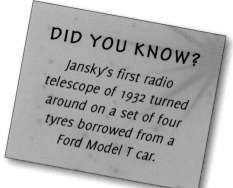

DID YOU KNOW?
Jansky's first radio telescope of 1932 turned around on a set of four tyres borrowed from a Ford Model T car.

◀ ATCA, the Australia Telescope Compact Array near Narrabri, New South Wales, has six radio telescope dishes, each 22 m across.

Arecibo RT

- **The world's largest** single-structure radio telescope is the Arecibo RT in the region of Arecibo, on the northern Caribbean island of Puerto Rico.

- **The enormous dish** is 305 m across and is set into a natural hollow in the landscape between hills.

- **The dish** is made from almost 38,000 panels of the metal aluminium, supported clear of the ground and adjustable on frames of steel girders, struts and cables.

- **The dish forms** part of the surface of a sphere or ball, unlike many other radio telescope dishes which have a surface that gradually changes its amount of curve, known as a parabola.

- **The whole dish** is fixed so the only way it can point at different parts of the sky is by Earth's daily spinning around and its yearly orbit around the Sun.

- **However the huge receiver** hanging above the dish can be moved below its platform to detect radio waves at different angles.

- **Sets of cables** suspend the platform and receiver, weighing 900 tonnes, 150 m above the centre of the dish.

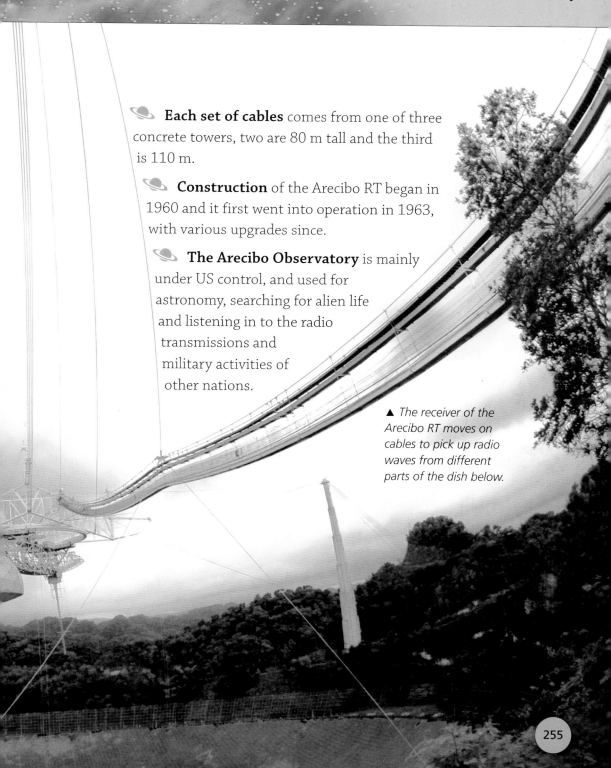

🪐 **Each set of cables** comes from one of three concrete towers, two are 80 m tall and the third is 110 m.

🪐 **Construction** of the Arecibo RT began in 1960 and it first went into operation in 1963, with various upgrades since.

🪐 **The Arecibo Observatory** is mainly under US control, and used for astronomy, searching for alien life and listening in to the radio transmissions and military activities of other nations.

▲ *The receiver of the Arecibo RT moves on cables to pick up radio waves from different parts of the dish below.*

Interferometry

🪐 **Energy in the form of waves**, especially radio, light and similar electromagnetic waves, has a feature called interference.

🪐 **If two waves** of the same wavelength travel together and their peaks and troughs line up, in effect they create one larger wave.

🪐 **But if the peak** of one wave lines up with the trough of the other, the interaction between them means the two waves effectively cancel each other out.

🪐 **If the two waves** are slightly different wavelengths, then in some regions their peaks gradually line up more and more and add together, then line up less and less and reduce each other.

▼ *ALMA, the Atacama Large Millimetre/sub-millimetre Array, consists of 66 radio telescope dishes in the Chilean Andes. Each dish receives very slightly different sets of waves which are compared to see how they have interfered with each other.*

These kinds of interactions, or interference, produce many effects seen in daily life, such as the coloured patches on soap film bubbles, coloured oily patches floating on water, and the rainbow colours on DVD or CD surfaces.

Interferometry is the study and measurement of interference, its causes, patterns and results, and it has many uses in astronomy and other sciences.

Several radio telescope dishes spaced far apart each receive slightly different timings of radio waves from space, for example, due to the curvature of the Earth.

Analyzing these sets of waves reveals their interference patterns and gives more details about their length, strength, source and other features.

Interferometry has led to the designs of telescopes called arrays, with several or many individual units spaced apart.

Radio array telescopes

● **Radio and other telescopes** with individual units spaced apart, but networked by computers, are called arrays. Arrays can detect a feature of waves called interference.

● **The Very Long Baseline Array** (VLBA) is made of ten telescope dishes scattered across the US. The effective total end-to-end distance is more than 8000 km.

● **Each individual dish** is 25 m across, weighs 220 tonnes and is linked to the Array Operations Centre in Socorro, New Mexico.

● **The VLBA** detects waves with wavelengths ranging from almost 30 cm down to just 3 mm, which is the microwave part of the wave spectrum.

● **The Karl G Jansky Very Large Array** (JVLA) is also located near Socorro and consists of 27 dishes, each 25 m across and weighing 210 tonnes.

🪐 **To detect various lengths** and strengths of waves, the Jansky Array dishes can move on a Y-shaped arrangement of rails, each arm of the Y measuring 21 km.

🪐 **The Atacama Large Millimeter Array** (ALMA) is sited in the Atacama Desert, along with several other observatories.

🪐 **ALMA** has 66 dishes, some 12 m across and weighing 110 tonnes, and others 7 m across. The array began work in 2011.

DID YOU KNOW?

The 66 ALMA dishes were carried to the remote Atacama site by two specially made haulage trucks, each 20 m long and 130 tonnes in weight.

▼ The 27-dish JVLA in New Mexico has studied planets forming around distant stars and also black holes, especially Sagittarius A* at the centre of the Milky Way.

259

Space telescopes

🪐 **In order to study the Universe** without interference from Earth's atmosphere, space telescopes are launched.

🪐 **Some of these space telescopes** are called space observatories since they have so much extra equipment in addition to the telescope itself.

🪐 **Some space telescopes** orbit Earth as satellites, while others orbit the Sun or make their own path through space.

🪐 **Away from Earth's atmosphere**, space telescopes and observatories do not suffer blurring, dust, artificial lights and other problems of the atmosphere.

🪐 **However space brings its own problems** such as risk of collision with meteoroids, huge extremes of temperature, and intense forms of radiation energy.

🪐 **Different space telescopes** study all the different forms of radiation that make up the electromagnetic spectrum.

🪐 **These include** low and high frequency radio waves, low and high frequency microwaves, infrared, visible light, ultraviolet, X-rays and gamma rays.

🪐 **Some space telescopes** can study various kinds of rays and waves, rather than just one kind such as visible light.

🪐 **The first space telescope** was Uhuru, sent up in 1970.

🪐 **Uhuru was first** of several space telescopes designed to map the entire sky for sources of X-rays.

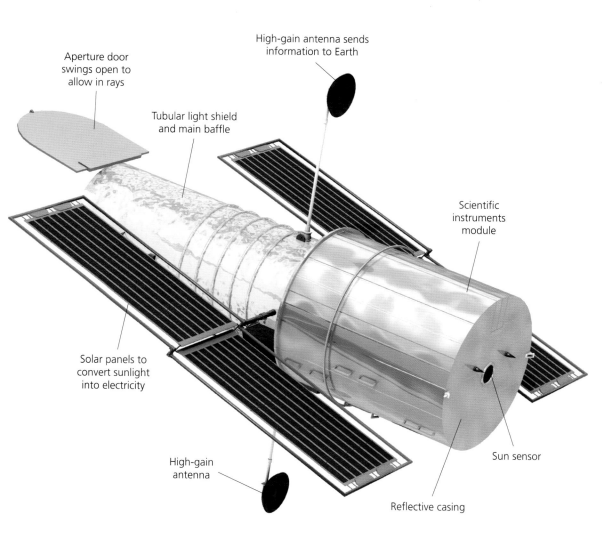

High-gain antenna sends
information to Earth

Aperture door
swings open to
allow in rays

Tubular light shield
and main baffle

Scientific
instruments
module

Solar panels to
convert sunlight
into electricity

High-gain
antenna

Sun sensor

Reflective casing

▲ *The best-known space telescope is the Hubble Space
Telescope, HST. It can detect clear images of faint objects in
space because it is above Earth's atmosphere.*

Microwave space telescopes

Microwaves are electromagnetic waves that are longer than most radio waves, but shorter than infrared rays. Their lengths range from about one metre to one millimetre.

▼ *COBE, NASA's Cosmic Background Explorer satellite, received microwaves and infrared rays at 100 different and very precise wavelengths.*

- **The first main space telescope** specially designed for microwaves was the Cosmic Background Explorer (COBE), launched into Earth orbit by NASA in 1989.

- **COBE is famous for detecting** microwaves coming from all directions in space, often called 'echoes of the Big Bang'.

- **In 2001 NASA sent up** the Wilkinson Microwave Anisotropy Probe (WMAP) as a successor to COBE. It continued to operate until 2010.

- **WMAP helped to confirm the echo** microwave background and allowed experts to find more information about the Big Bang, the start of the Universe, and the roles of dark matter and dark energy.

- **WMAP measurements** place the Big Bang at 13.77 billion (13,770 million) years ago, give or take a few million years.

- **WMAP has a specialized orbit** at a position called L2 (Lagrange Point 2). This point is about 1.5 million km from the side of Earth facing away from the Sun. Here the gravities of the Sun and Earth are balanced.

- **The Planck space telescope** was launched by the European Space Agency in 2009. It is named after famous German physicist Max Planck (1858–1947).

- **Planck continued the work** of COBE and WMAP, mapping the cosmic microwave background and also studying infrared waves, until 2013. Its measurements suggest the Universe contains 26 percent dark matter.

Infrared space telescopes

🪐 **Infrared waves** are electromagnetic waves that are shorter than microwaves but longer than light waves – about one to 0.0007 mm (1000 to 0.7 micrometres).

🪐 **Infrared waves** are known as thermal radiation because they carry what we feel as heat energy.

🪐 **The Herschel Space Observatory** was launched in 2009 by NASA and the European Space Observatory, and continued its work until 2013.

🪐 **Herschel was a very large craft** more than 7 m long and 4 m wide, weighing 315 kg.

🪐 **It had a bowl-shaped mirror** 3.5 m across to collect the incredibly faint infrared or heat waves coming from the most distant and coolest stars, galaxies and even space dust.

🪐 **In 2003** the Spitzer Space Telescope (SST) was placed in orbit around the Sun, at about the same distance as Earth but trailing behind.

🪐 **Spitzer was named after US astronomer** Lyman Spitzer (1914–1997), who was one of the first to suggest telescopes could work in space.

▶ *Herschel took this image of Orion A, a star-forming nebula some 1500 light-years from Earth. Like all infrared images it is in effect a 'heat picture'.*

🪐 **Like other infrared space observatories**, Spitzter's sensors are cooled by an enormous amount, to just 30°C above absolute zero.

🪐 **Spitzer was one** of the first telescopes to detect evidence of exoplanets – planets orbiting stars other than our Sun.

🪐 **The Wide-field Infrared Survey Explorer** (WISE) was launched by NASA in 2009.

🪐 **One of WISE's tasks** is to scan for asteroids that might come near to, or even collide with, Earth.

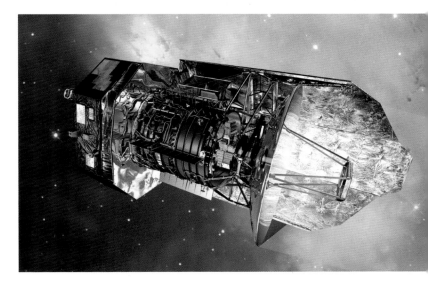

▲ *Herschel was a very large craft launched by an Ariane 5 rocket. It exceeded its planned life by six months. In the end it ran out of the liquid helium coolant needed to keep it so cold, just 2°C above absolute zero, so that it was more sensitive to faint infrared.*

265

Optical space telescopes

🪐 **Optical, or light**, space telescopes detect the same electromagnetic waves as our eyes – light or visible light.

🪐 **Optical telescopes** include the famous Hubble Space Telescope.

🪐 **The Gaia Space Observatory**, launched in 2013 by the European Space Agency, aims to carry out a massive survey of space.

▼ *Three views of the 4.7-m-long Kepler 'planet-hunter' telescope. It has just one photometer, for visible light, but this is incredibly sensitive.*

● **Gaia's tasks** include mapping the positions and distances of millions of stars in the Milky Way, as well as thousands of new asteroids, comets and quasars.

● **The US Kepler space observatory**, launched into space in 2009, is specifically designed to detect planets orbiting stars other than our Sun, called exoplanets.

● **However by 2013** two of Kepler's four reaction wheels, which manoeuvre and point the craft, had failed.

● **By 2014** organizers altered Kepler's mission to search for exoplanets in a more limited way but it still also carried out other observations.

● **BRITE is a group or constellation** of six tiny observing satellites launched in 2013 and 2014 from various locations in India, Russia and China.

● **Each BRITE craft** is box-shaped and just 20 cm across. One was lost at launch, but the others went into operation.

● **Organized by Canada**, Austria and Poland, the BRITE nanosatellites are designed to study very bright stars.

267

Ultraviolet space telescopes

- **Ultraviolet or UV waves** in the electromagnetic spectrum are shorter than light waves but longer than X-rays. The shortest are just 10 nanometres (0.000,01 mm) in length.

- **Space telescopes** that have studied ultraviolet rays from the stars include the International Ultraviolet Explorer (IUE), 1978–1996, and the Extreme Ultraviolet Explorer (EUVE), 1992–2001.

- **Hisaki was put into Low Earth Orbit** in 2013 by Japan's Aerospace Agency, JAXA.

- **Known at first** as the Spectroscopic Planet Observatory for Recognition of Interaction of Atmosphere (SPRINT-A), Hisaki studied the atmospheres of planets in the Solar System.

- **Also in 2013**, NASA launched the Interface Region Imaging Spectrograph (IRIS) satellite into Earth orbit.

- **IRIS observes the Sun**, in particular the ultraviolet waves coming from the surface and just below, in the region known as the chromosphere, where the temperature is up to 20,000°C.

- **Among the discoveries of IRIS** are newly discovered Sun features known as plasma jets, nano-flares and heat-bombs.

- **Swift is a multi-wavelength** space telescope with several sets of equipment to detect visible light, UV, and also the shorter waves of X-rays and gamma rays.

- **Swift went into Low Earth Orbit** in 2004 and has continued to work far beyond its expected life of two years.

Swift's UV equipment senses the afterglow of massive events called gamma ray bursts, coming from giant stars that collapse into neutron stars or black holes.

▼ *Swift is 5.6 m long and weighs 615 kg. Its name comes from its speedy reaction to swing around and point at likely regions sending out waves.*

Hubble Space Telescope

⭐ **The Hubble Space Telescope**, HST, has advanced astronomy and space science more than almost any other single piece of equipment. It is named after US astronomer Edwin Hubble, and has taken many thousands of images.

⭐ **It was launched** by the space shuttle Discovery in 1990 and continues to orbit every 95.6 minutes at an average height of 555 km above sea level.

⭐ **The HST weighs** 11 tonnes and is 13.2 m long and 4.2 m wide.

⭐ **It detects mainly visible light** and the two kinds of radiation either side of those wavelengths, being near infrared (slightly longer waves) and near ultraviolet (shorter).

⭐ **The HST has a reflecting** telescope with a mirror 2.4 m across.

⭐ **When first used**, astronomers noticed that the images being sent back were slightly blurred. It was discovered that the main mirror had been made slightly to the wrong shape, by about 0.002 mm (2 micrometres). The telescope was in effect 'short-sighted'.

⭐ **In 1993** during space shuttle mission STS–61 Endeavour captured the HST and made alterations needing five long spacewalks. The changes were all successful and the HST could now see into the depths of the Universe.

⭐ **There were another** four servicing missions to the HST, the last in 2009, to install updated cameras and other equipment.

▶ *Shuttle mission STS-61 carried out the first update of the Hubble Space Telescope, in particular to cure its 'short sight'. Here astronaut Story Musgrave on the robot arm installs new magnetometers, with Jeffrey Hoffman in the shuttle's payload bay.*

DID YOU KNOW?

The HST will gradually be replaced by the James Webb Space Telescope probably some time around 2020.

X-ray and gamma telescopes

🪐 **Gamma rays** are the shortest waves in the range or spectrum of electromagnetic waves. About one billion (1000 million) end to end only measure one millimetre.

🪐 **X-rays are slightly** longer than gamma rays, with one million fitting into one millimetre.

🪐 **Both X-rays and gamma rays** carry large amounts of energy and much information about their sources.

🪐 **NASA's Compton Gamma Ray Observatory** (CGRO) was in Low Earth Orbit from 1991 to 2000 and returned enormous amounts of information about gamma rays and X-rays coming from space.

🪐 **The CGRO** detected hundreds of new gamma ray sources that include possible clouds of antimatter. It also found that thunderclouds here on Earth give off gamma rays.

🪐 **X-rays from space** are blocked by Earth's atmosphere so X-ray space observatories are the only way to gain information about them.

🪐 **The Chandra X-ray Observatory** (CXO) was put into a very elongated or elliptical Earth orbit in 1999. It far outlived its original working life of five years, clocking up 15 years in 2014.

🪐 **Discoveries by Chandra** include a small galaxy being absorbed or 'cannibalized' by a bigger one, and X-rays from the supermassive black hole, Sagittarius A*, at the Milky Way's centre. This black hole flared up greatly in 2015, perhaps as it swallowed a body such as an asteroid.

◀ NASA'S 10-m-long NuSTAR (Nuclear Spectroscopic Telescope Array) was launched in 2012. Its X-ray and other detectors search for supermassive black holes, the highest-energy particles and how chemical elements are forged in supernovae.

James Webb Space Telescope

🪐 **The Hubble Space Telescope**, launched in 1990, is expected to be replaced sometime around 2018–2020 by the James Webb Space Telescope (JWST).

🪐 **The telescope** is named after James E Webb (1906–1992), a prominent member of NASA from 1961 to 1968 who played a major role in the Apollo manned moon missions and research programmes.

🪐 **The JWST will detect** visible and infrared rays using a mirror 6.5 m across – five times the area of Hubble's mirror.

🪐 **The mirror is made up** of 18 hexagonal (six-sided) units coated with gold.

🪐 **To sense infrared** or heat rays, the JWST must be very cold. It is protected from the Sun by a massive heat shield measuring 20 m by 7.2 m. The whole craft is kept at a temperature below minus 220°C, which is less than 50° above absolute zero.

🪐 **Among the JWST's aims** are to study light from the first and now most distant stars and galaxies formed after the Big Bang, and how galaxies begin and evolve.

🪐 **Further aims** include studying how stars and their planets form, and also how life might appear and evolve.

🪐 **The expected cost** of the whole JWST programme has increased 20 times, from about US$0.5 billion (500 million) in 1997 to probably more than US$10 billion (10,000 million) by its completion.

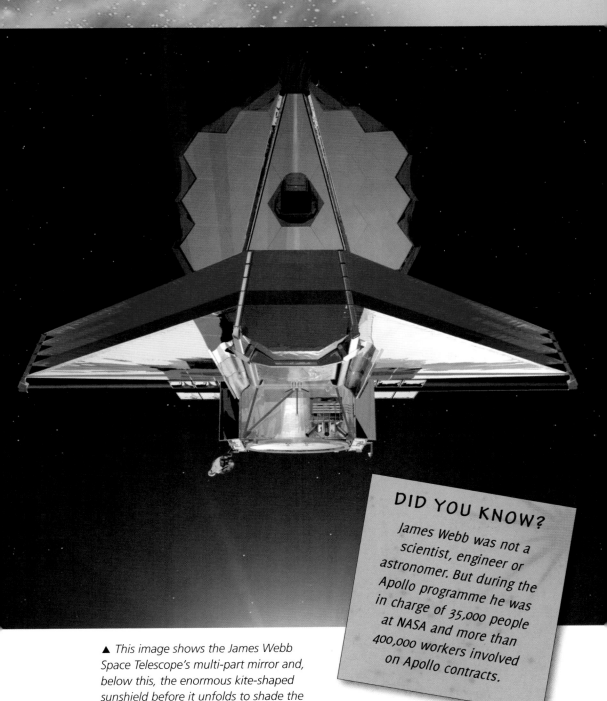

▲ This image shows the James Webb Space Telescope's multi-part mirror and, below this, the enormous kite-shaped sunshield before it unfolds to shade the craft from the Sun's heat.

DID YOU KNOW?

James Webb was not a scientist, engineer or astronomer. But during the Apollo programme he was in charge of 35,000 people at NASA and more than 400,000 workers involved on Apollo contracts.

275

Ancient astronomy

🪐 **Many ancient cultures** were deeply interested in stargazing and spent much time thinking about the Sun, Moon and other objects in the sky.

🪐 **With no interference** from artificial lights, except from a camp fire or perhaps oil lamps, many more objects were visible in the night sky compared to modern times.

▶ The 'Venus tablet' records astronomical observations of Venus made over 21 years.

- **Many early cultures** imagined gods and spirits inhabiting a starry realm. They viewed celestial events such as eclipses, shooting stars (meteor showers) and comets as supernatural premonitions.

- **Knowledge of the movements** of the Sun, Moon and other space bodies also had many practical uses in the daily lives of ancient cultures.

- **Early astronomy** led to organized calendars for crop planting, harvest and other events, and to navigation aids on journeys across unfamiliar lands and seas.

- **The Warren Field calendar** in Aberdeenshire, Scotland, dates to 10,000 years ago. Its twelve pits have positions linked to the Moon's phases and winter solstice (midwinter day).

- **The huge stone monument** of Stonehenge in Wiltshire, England, was aligned with both the Sun's position at the summer and winter solstices. More than 4000 years old, it had circles of huge upright stones.

- **The ancient Babylonians** (in what is now Iraq) were the first to compile, calculate and record celestial events in a scientific way, using their cuneiform writing system.

- **The Babylonian 'Venus tablet'**, describing the motions of planet Venus, is one of the earliest known astronomical texts, going back at least 3500 years ago.

Hipparchus

🪐 **Hipparchus of Nicaea** was a Greek astronomer who lived in the 2nd century BC, and died in 127 BC.

🪐 **The framework for astronomy** was created by Hipparchus.

🪐 **Hipparchus' ideas** were almost lost until they were rescued by Greek astronomer, Ptolemy (90 AD–168 AD). They were developed into a system that lasted 1500 years until they were overthrown by the ideas of Copernicus (1473–1543).

🪐 **Ancient Babylonian** records brought back by Alexander the Great from his conquests helped Hipparchus to make his observations of the stars.

🪐 **Hipparchus** was the first astronomer to measure Earth's distance to the Sun.

▶ *Hipparchus carried out his observations at Rhodes. He was the first to pinpoint the geographical position of places by latitude and longitude.*

◄ *Some of Hipparchus'
knowledge of stars came
from the Sumerians, who
wrote on clay tablets.*

🪐 **He also made an early star list**, and was the first to identify
the constellations systematically and to assess stars in terms
of magnitude.

🪐 **Hipparchus discovered** that the positions of the stars on
the equinoxes (21 March and 23 September) slowly shift
around, taking 26,000 years to
return to their original place.
This is known as precession,
due to a slight 'wobble' in the
Earth's axis of rotation.

DID YOU KNOW?

The mathematics of
trigonometry is thought
to have been invented
by Hipparchus.

Ptolemy

🪐 **The most famous of the ancient astronomers** was Greek-Roman Claudius Ptolemy. He revived, extended, and publicized the work of earlier Greek astronomers, especially Hipparchus.

🪐 **Ptolemy lived and worked** in the North African city of Alexandria during the first half of the 2nd century AD. According to tradition he died there in 168 AD at the age of 78.

🪐 **Ptolemy's astronomical work** was published in a book entitled *The Mathematical Collection*, but which became known in Greek as *The Great Astronomer*.

🪐 **Islamic scholars of the Middle Ages** referred to Ptolemy's book as the *Megiste* (*Masterwork*), and it is now generally known as the *Almagest*.

🪐 **The *Almagest* is divided into 13 chapters**. The first six chapters are concerned with the motion of the Sun and Moon. Chapters seven and eight deal with the stars and the constellations and the final five chapters are about the planets.

🪐 **Ptolemy followed Hipparchus in believing** that Earth was at the centre of the Universe, and this Ptolemaic viewpoint lasted until the Copernican Revolution overthrew it.

🪐 **Ptolemy also believed** that the Sun, stars and planets were embedded in series of concentric transparent crystal spheres that surrounded the Earth.

🪐 **According to Ptolemy**, the sequence of heavenly bodies from the Earth outwards was: the Moon, Mercury, Venus, the Sun, Mars, Jupiter, Saturn and the stars.

▲ *Ptolemy's conception of the Universe, with Earth at the centre, was accepted for more than 1000 years until overturned by the work of Nicolaus Copernicus.*

🪐 **Ptolemy extended Hipparchus' star catalogue** to include a total of 1022 stars and defined 48 of the constellations that are now internationally recognized.

🪐 **In a separate book** he prepared a calendar showing the times of rising and setting of certain prominent stars during morning and evening twilight.

Copernicus

◀ *'The Earth,'* wrote Copernicus, *'carrying the Moon's path, passes in a great orbit among the other planets in an annual revolution around the Sun.'*

🪐 **Until the 16th century** most people thought Earth was the centre of the Universe and that everything – Moon, Sun, planets and stars – revolved around it. This is called the geocentric view.

🪐 **Nicolaus Copernicus** (1473–1543) was the astronomer who first suggested that the Sun was the Solar System's centre, and that Earth went around it. This is known as the heliocentric view.

🪐 **Copernicus had an extensive education** at the best universities in Poland and Italy. He studied astronomy, astrology, various languages, medicine and law.

🪐 **In his book**, *De revolutionibus orbium coelestium* (*On the Revolutions of the Heavenly Spheres*), Copernicus described his new ideas.

🪐 **The Roman Catholic Church** banned Copernicus' book for about 140 years.

🪐 **Copernicus' ideas** came mainly from studying ancient astronomy.

🪐 **His main clue** came from the way the planets, seen from Earth, seem to perform a backward loop through the sky every now and then.

- **The first proof of Copernicus' theory** came in 1610, when Galileo saw, through a telescope, moons revolving around Jupiter.

- **The change in ideas** that was brought about by Copernicus is known as the Copernican Revolution.

▼ *Copernicus was the first to realize that the Sun is at the centre of the Solar System, and the planets orbit around it.*

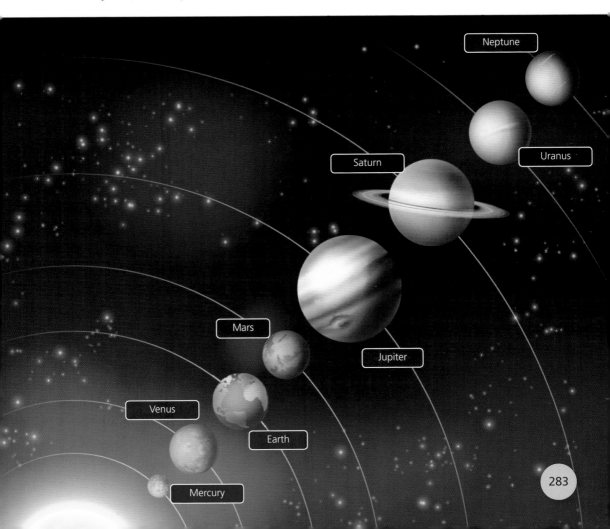

Neptune

Uranus

Saturn

Mars

Jupiter

Venus

Earth

Mercury

283

Brahe

🪐 **Wealthy Danish nobleman** Tycho Brahe (1546–1601) was the last great European astronomer to work without a telescope, which came into use a few years after he died.

🪐 **Brahe loved to catalogue space objects**, calculate their movements, and work out their mathematical relationships.

🪐 **Copernicus' great book** *On the Revolutions of the Heavenly Spheres* was published in 1543, just before Brahe was born. Brahe grew up with these new controversial ideas as well as the long-established work of Ptolemy.

🪐 **Brahe owned Hven**, a small island between Sweden and Denmark. Here from the mid 1570s he built observatories and developed high-quality astronomical instruments.

🪐 **In 1572** Brahe observed a supernova (exploding star), since named SN 1572, and suspected it was far away. Working from his huge numbers of observations, he began to visualize space objects as much more remote than people believed.

🪐 **He developed his own view** of the Universe as geo-heliocentric, in which most objects orbited the Sun, but the Sun along with the Moon orbited the Earth.

🪐 **In 1597** Brahe moved to Prague as court astronomer to Holy Roman Emperor Rudolf II, where the young astronomer Johannes Kepler became an assistant.

DID YOU KNOW?
Brahe was famous for wearing a false nose, probably of brass, after his was sliced off in a sword duel.

🪐 **Kepler later used** many of Brahe's records in the Rudolphine Tables, published in 1627.

🪐 **The Moon crater Tycho** is named in his honour.

▼ *Brahe devised various complex orbits for planets and moons, some around the Sun and others around Earth – here the latter.*

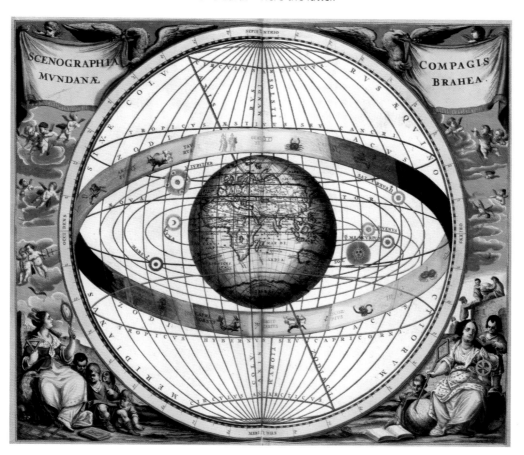

Galileo

Galileo Galilei (1564–1642) was a great Italian mathematician, astronomer, engineer and scientific philosopher.

In 1581 Galileo observed how a lamp in Pisa Cathedral, swinging like a pendulum, took the same time for a small swing as a large one. This began his interest in motion, forces and gravity.

▼ *Using his own-made telescopes, Galileo made many observations for the first time, such as the Milky Way consisting not of gas but of myriad stars.*

- **Galileo's experiments with balls** rolling down slopes founded our understanding of how gravity makes things accelerate.

- **When the telescope was invented** in about 1608, Galileo made his own improved versions from 1609. He first looked at the Moon, Venus and Jupiter.

- **Galileo described his observations** of space in a book called *The Starry Messenger*, published in 1610.

- **Through his telescope**, Galileo saw that Jupiter has four moons. He also saw that Venus has phases, as Earth's Moon does.

- **Jupiter's moons and Venus' phases** were the first visible evidence of Copernicus' theory. Galileo soon came to believe this.

- **Galileo supported the Copernican theory**, which was declared a heresy by the Catholic Church in 1616.

- **Threatened with torture**, Galileo was forced to deny that the Earth orbits the Sun. He was then kept under house arrest until he died.

- **In 1992**, 350 years after his death, the Catholic Church admitted it had been wrong and apologized for its treatment of Galileo.

DID YOU KNOW?
Galileo has had more than a dozen moons, asteroids, craters, spacecraft and other astronomical objects named in his honour.

Kepler

🪐 **German astronomer Johannes Kepler** (1571–1630) discovered the basic rules that govern the way in which the planets move.

🪐 **Kepler got his ideas** from studying the movement of Mars.

🪐 **Before Kepler's discoveries**, it was thought that the planets moved in circles.

🪐 **Kepler discovered** that the true shape of the planets' orbits is elliptical (a type of oval). This is Kepler's first law.

🪐 **Kepler's second law** is that the speed of a planet through space varies according to its distance from the Sun.

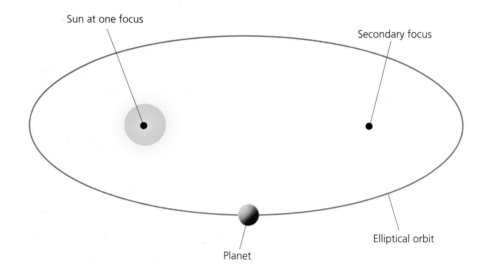

Sun at one focus

Secondary focus

Elliptical orbit

Planet

▲ *Kepler discovered that planets have an elliptical orbit around the Sun. The Sun is not at the centre, but at one of the focuses.*

▶ *Despite almost losing his eyesight and the use of his hands through smallpox at the age of three, Johannes Kepler became an assistant to the great Danish astronomer Tycho Brahe, and took over his work when Brahe died.*

🪐 **A planet moves fastest** when its orbit brings it nearest to the Sun. This point is known as its perihelion. It moves slowest when it is furthest from the Sun, called its aphelion.

🪐 **The third law** concerns a planet's period, that is, the time it takes to complete its yearly orbit of the Sun – the planet's year. This depends on its distance from the Sun.

🪐 **Kepler's third law states** that the square of a planet's period is proportional to the cube of its average distance from the Sun.

🪐 **Kepler also believed** that the planets made music as they moved, he called this the music of the spheres.

Huygens

🪐 **A scientist with many interests** and innovations to his name, Christiaan Huygens (1629–1695) was born into a wealthy Dutch family and received a varied high-quality education.

🪐 **As a student** he became especially interested in mathematics, mechanics and natural philosophy. In the 1650s he studied lenses and telescopes, and made lenses and eyepieces to his own novel design. He took an increasing interest in astronomy.

▲ *In his book* Cosmotheoros, *Huygens suggested that water was necessary for life on other planets – a view still held today.*

🪐 **In 1655**, with his more powerful telescopes, Huygens was able to see that Saturn had a ring or rings around it.

🪐 **Also in 1655** Huygens identified Titan, Saturn's largest moon and the second-biggest moon in the Solar System.

🪐 **Huygens continued to improve** lenses and telescopes into his old age.

🪐 **Other discoveries** made by Huygens include the different parts of the Orion Nebula as well as several new stars and nebulae.

🪐 **The possibility** of extraterrestrial or alien life also fascinated Huygens, as described in his 1698 book *Cosmotheoros*.

🪐 **In addition** to astronomy, Huygens devised a wave theory of light, advanced laws of motion and mechanics, invented the pendulum clock and watch balance spring, and greatly improved the designs of many kinds of clocks and timepieces.

🪐 **The lander Huygens** of the Cassini-Huygens space mission, which touched down on Titan in 2005, was named after him.

🪐 **Huygens has also been honoured** with an asteroid, Martian crater and Moon mountain all named after him.

▶ *Huygens made many of his discoveries, including Titan, using improved telescopes he built with his brother Constantijn Huygens.*

Cassini

 **Giovanni Cassini** (1625–1712), also known as Jean-Dominique Cassini, was an Italian scientist specializing in mathematics, mechanics, engineering and astronomy.

 **As a student**, Cassini showed a great talent for devising and using astronomical instruments as well as forecasting astrological events. In 1650, aged just 25, he became professor of astronomy at Bologna University, Italy, then one of the leading institutions in Europe.

 **In 1669** Cassini moved to Paris to become director of the Paris Observatory and court astronomer to the 'Sun King' Louis XIV.

 **Many of Cassini's discoveries** were related to the planet Saturn. Between 1671 and 1684 he identified four of its moons: Iapetus, Rhea, Tethys and Dione.

 **The Cassini Division** gap between parts of Saturn's ring system was another of his findings. He discovered it in 1675.

 **Mars also interested Cassini**. He made detailed studies of the planet's surface patterns and timed its rotations (Martian days).

 **With colleagues**, Cassini helped to work out the distance from Earth to Mars, thereby giving a sense of scale to the Solar System.

 **Jupiter was another favourite**. Cassini described its Great Red Spot and rotation speed, noting this was different at the equator and near the poles.

 **The orbiter** Cassini of the Cassini-Huygens space mission, which reached Saturn in 2004, is named after him.

▼ *This image of Saturn's rings, with the Cassini Division the main gap with a slight greyish tinge within, was taken by the Cassini spacecraft.*

DID YOU KNOW?

Like Huygens, Cassini has craters on the Moon and Mars, and an asteroid, named in his honour.

Newton

- **Isaac Newton** (1642–1727) discovered laws that govern the force of gravity and motion.

- **Newton's discovery of gravity** showed why planets orbit the Sun.

- **He realized** that a planet's orbit depends on its mass and its distance from the Sun.

- **The farther apart** and the lighter two objects are, the weaker the pull of gravity is between them.

▼ *In the 1660s Newton discovered that sunlight can be split into a spectrum made of all the colours of the rainbow. This led to the science of spectroscopy, much used in space science.*

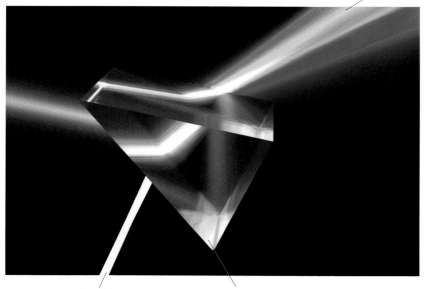

Spectrum of colours

White light   Prism

🪐 **To calculate the pull of gravity** between two objects, multiply their masses together, then divide the total by the square of the distance between them.

🪐 **This calculation allows astronomers** to predict the movement of every planet, star and galaxy in the Universe.

🪐 **Using Newton's formula for gravity** (and more lately Einstein's work), astronomers have detected new stars and planets, including Neptune, from the effect of their gravity on other space objects.

🪐 **Newton's three laws of motion** showed how movements of objects in space can be calculated using celestial mechanics. This became known as the 'clockwork Universe', although Einstein's work has replaced some of these ideas.

🪐 **Newton's book** *Philosophiæ Naturalis Principia Mathematica* ('Mathematical Principles of Natural Philosophy') of 1687, usually known as the *Principia*, explained his many advances.

▶ *Newton was made Lucasian professor of mathematics at Cambridge University in 1669, where he studied how and why things in our Universe move as they do.*

Halley

🪐 **English scientist and astronomer** Edmund Halley (1656–1742) is perhaps most famous for the comet named after him.

🪐 **However Halley was one of the leading scientists** and explorers of his day, and made many discoveries.

🪐 **Halley became one of the youngest** ever members of the Royal Society aged 22.

🪐 **His interests ranged** from detailed studies of the Moon and other astronomical objects to the make-up of Earth, its rocks, atmosphere, climate and magnetism.

🪐 **Halley also made advances** in mechanics, motion, gravity and mathematics.

🪐 **He travelled around Europe** and across the Atlantic, setting up an observatory on the remote island of Saint Helena. In 1676 he observed Mercury passing in front of the Sun and suggested ways of using these events – transits – to calculate distances in the Solar System.

▶ *Halley collaborated with Isaac Newton, Robert Hooke, Christopher Wren, John Flamsteed, Giovanni Cassini, Johannes Hevelius and many others.*

- **After discussing gravity** and motion with Isaac Newton, Halley urged him to publish his work, which Newton did in 1687 as the *Principia*.

- **Costs for publishing** the *Principia* were paid by Halley, and it is now regarded as one of the most important scientific works of all time.

- **In 1705**, after noticing visits by a comet in 1456, 1531, 1607 and 1682, Halley predicted its return in 1758 – when it became known as Halley's comet.

- **In 1720** Halley became the second British Astronomer Royal when he succeeded John Flamsteed, and he held that title until his death aged 85.

Herschel

🪐 **William Herschel** (1738–1822) was a German musician who became the King's astronomer in England and built his own powerful telescopes.

🪐 **Until Herschel's time**, astronomers thought that there were only six planets, including Earth, orbiting the Sun.

🪐 **The other five known planets** at that time were Mercury, Venus, Mars, Jupiter and Saturn.

🪐 **Uranus, the seventh planet**, was discovered by William Herschel in 1781.

🪐 **At first Herschel thought** that the dot of light he could see through his telescope was a nebula or comet. When he looked again four days later, it had moved against the background of stars, which meant it must be in the Solar System. He realized that it was a new planet.

🪐 **He wanted to name** the planet George, after King George III, but Uranus was eventually chosen, after the ancient Greek god of the sky.

▶ *William Herschel was one of the greatest astronomers. With the help of his sister, Caroline, he discovered Uranus in 1781. He later identified two of the moons of Uranus and two of Saturn.*

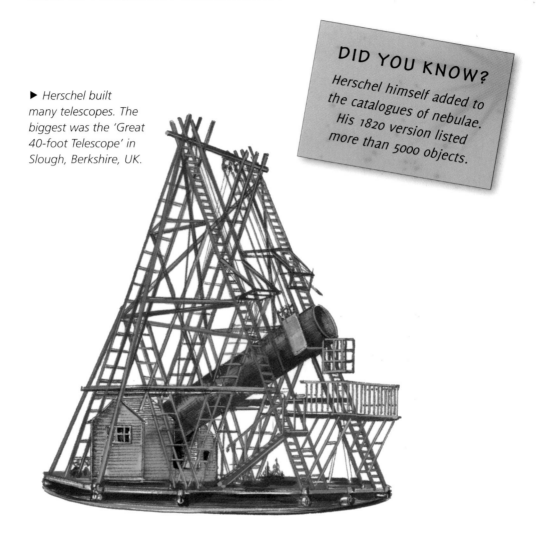

▶ *Herschel built many telescopes. The biggest was the 'Great 40-foot Telescope' in Slough, Berkshire, UK.*

🪐 **Herschel's sister, Caroline** (1750–1848), was his partner in his discoveries. She was also a great astronomer who discovered eight comets and produced excellent catalogues of stars and nebulae.

🪐 **John, Herschel's son,** catalogued the stars of the Southern Hemisphere.

Einstein

🪐 **The great mathematician-scientist** Albert Einstein (1879–1955) is known for devising two theories of relativity.

🪐 **Special relativity** shows that all measurements are relative, including time, space and speed. In other words, time and space and speed depend on where and when they are measured.

🪐 **The fastest thing in the Universe**, light, always travels at the same speed, no matter where you are or how fast you are going.

▲ *In his later years, Einstein strove to find a 'grand theory of everything'.*

🪐 **Special relativity also shows**, among other events, that as things travel faster, they seem to become shorter and heavier.

🪐 **The theory of general relativity** includes the idea of special relativity, but also describes how gravity works. It led to the notion of four dimensions: three of physical space (up-down, left-right, forwards-backwards), and time. This is known as 'space-time'.

🪐 **General relativity predicts** that light rays from stars are bent by the gravitational pull of stars and other huge objects that they pass. The star does this by stretching space-time.

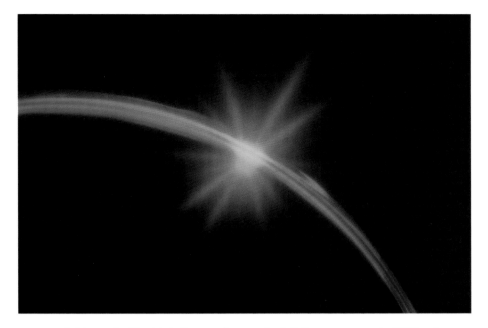

▲ *Evidence for Einstein's theory of general relativity was proven in 1919, when light rays from distant stars, just grazing the Sun on their way to Earth, were measured during an eclipse and shown to be bent.*

🪐 **Einstein overturned the idea** that time is the same everywhere. He was the first to show that time is relative. It depends entirely on how you measure it – and you can only measure it relative to something else. So time can pass faster or slower.

🪐 **Relativity shows that as speed increases**, time slows down. So for astronauts orbiting Earth, time passes very slightly slower than for people on Earth.

Hubble

- **Edwin Hubble** (1889–1953) was an American who trained in law at the Universities of Chicago and Oxford, and was also a great boxer before he turned to astronomy.

- **Until the early 20th century**, astronomers thought that the Milky Way galaxy was all there was in the Universe.

- **In the 1920s**, Hubble showed that the fuzzy patches of light once thought to be nebulae (interstellar clouds of gas and dust) were in fact other galaxies far beyond the Milky Way.

- **In 1929, Hubble measured** the distances of 20 galaxies and showed that they were all moving away from the Earth.

- **Red shift** – the 'stretching' of light objects moving away from an observer – showed Hubble that the farther away a galaxy is, the faster it is moving.

- **The ratio of a galaxy's distance** to the speed it is moving away from Earth is now known as Hubble's Law.

- **Hubble's Law** showed that the Universe is getting bigger and so must have started very small. This led to the idea of the Big Bang.

- **Hubble's constant** is a measurement of the rate at which the Universe is expanding.

- **In the 1930s**, Hubble showed that on the largest scale the Universe is isotropic, that is, it looks the same in all directions no matter where you observe from. This also implies the Universe has no centre and no edges.

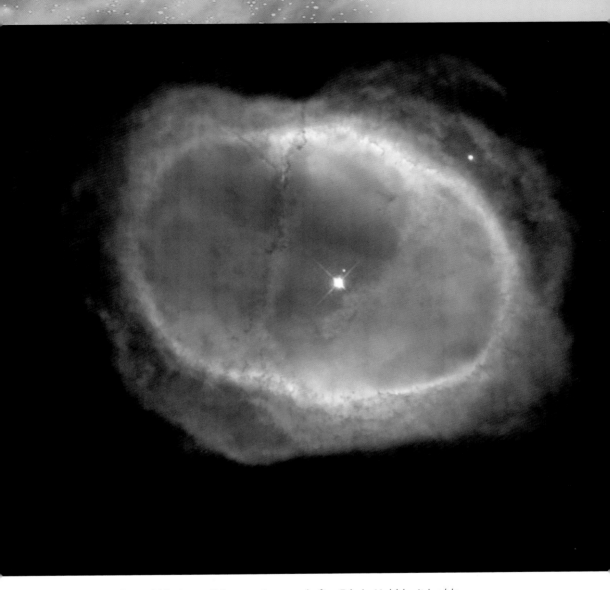

▲ *The Hubble Space Telescope is named after Edwin Hubble. It is able to see space objects, such as planetary nebulae, Nebula NGC 3132, shown here, in great detail.*

Sagan

🪐 **American Carl Sagan** (1934–1996) was not only a noted astronomer and all-round space scientist – he was also a great popularizer of space in general.

🪐 **Sagan wrote many books** and presented several successful TV series for the general public, on the excitement of space and its exploration.

🪐 **Among Sagan's specialties** were astrophysics and astrobiology, including the origins and evolution of life on Earth, possible life elsewhere in the Universe, and the search for it.

▼ Carl Sagan was a charismatic speaker and much in demand, especially when campaigning for money to fund space research.

With oxygen in its atmosphere, and possibly liquid water under its icy surface, Jupiter's moon Europa (foreground) is one of the likeliest places in the Solar System for some kind of life.

Planets Venus, Mars, Jupiter and Saturn fascinated Sagan. He speculated that some form of living matter might survive in the clouds of the latter two gas giants.

Sagan also proposed that Saturn's moon Titan and Jupiter's moon Europa might have liquids on the surface – a medium in which life could survive.

Cloud-shrouded Venus, suggested Sagan, was incredibly hot due to a runaway greenhouse effect.

Sagan also foresaw that Earth might have its own 'greenhouse effect', another speculation since verified.

The epic 13-part TV series *Cosmos* (1980) was co-written and presented by Sagan and shown in more than 100 countries.

***Cosmos* introduced the wonders of astronomy** and space to millions of people around the world and won numerous awards for popularizing science.

In addition, Sagan wrote hundreds of scientific papers and reports. His ideas on astronomy, space, the philosophy of science, and humanity's place in the Universe were greatly admired – even

Hawking

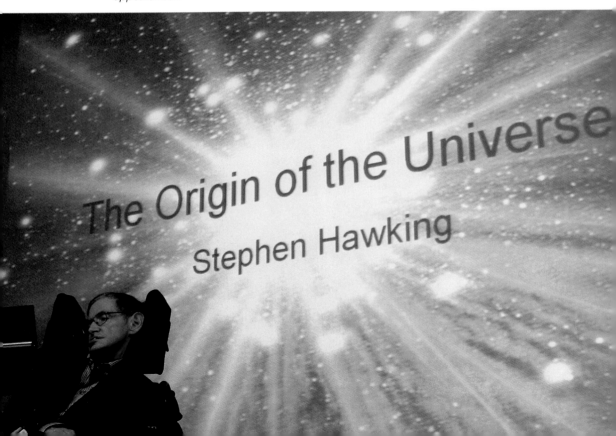

- **For many people**, English scientist Stephen Hawking (1942–) is the greatest celebrity associated with space and astronomy today.

- **However, his complex ideas** and mathematical logic can seem impossibly difficult to understand.

- **Based in Cambridge**, England, Hawking is especially involved in science on the grandest scale. He specializes in cosmology – the study of the Universe – its make-up, past and future.

▼ *Advances in communications technology have given Stephen Hawking the ability to deliver lectures and addresses at his much anticipated personal appearances.*

The Origin of the Universe

Stephen Hawking

🪐 **Despite living with the rare nerve-muscle condition** ALS (amyotrophic lateral sclerosis or motor neuron disease), Hawking has played an exceptionally full and active part in cosmology, astronomy, space research, and connected areas of science.

🪐 **In the 1960s** Hawking became interested in the then-novel idea of black holes and how to explain them using mathematics.

🪐 **Further work** followed on the Big Bang and origins of the Universe, and its likely fate – if indeed the Universe had a beginning or will have an end.

🪐 *A Brief History of Time* (1988), Hawking's popular book on cosmology and space science, has been an enormous bestseller.

🪐 **Hawking has worked** to link cosmological events, gravity and relativity with quantum mechanics, which applies at the tiniest level of atoms and their subatomic particles.

🪐 **In 2005** Hawking co-authored another bestseller, *A Briefer History of Time*, to update his earlier book.

🪐 **Hawking was appointed** Lucasian Professor of Mathematics in 1979. This is one of science's most prestigious posts, once held by Isaac Newton. According to the conditions of the appointment, he retired in 2009.

DID YOU KNOW?

Stephen Hawking has received more than 100 awards, medals, honorary positions and other distinctions from around the world.

Exploring space

Dawn of space travel

- **For centuries**, people imagined they could travel away from Earth into the realms of the gods, spirits and heavens – although they had no scientific understanding of what was out there.

- **With the beginnings** of scientific astronomy in the 16th century, more realistic ideas about space travel began to arise.

- **Popular stories of space travel** began in Europe with science fiction works such as Jules Verne's *From the Earth to the Moon* in 1865 and H G Wells' *The War of the Worlds* from 1898.

- **In 1903** Russian teacher-scientist Konstantin Tsiolkovsky published *Exploration of Outer Space by Means of Rocket Devices*; he was well ahead of his time.

- **In the 1920s** early experiments with rockets took place in the USA and Russia.

DID YOU KNOW?

The name of the first space traveller, Laika, refers to a husky-like breed of dog in Russian.

▶ *Laika, the first living creature in space, travelled in the Soviet spacecraft, Sputnik 2.*

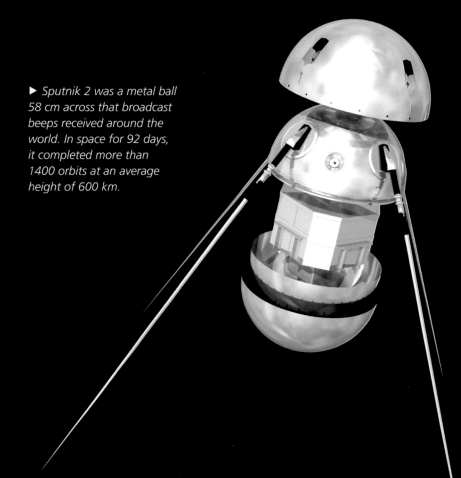

▶ *Sputnik 2 was a metal ball 58 cm across that broadcast beeps received around the world. In space for 92 days, it completed more than 1400 orbits at an average height of 600 km.*

🪐 **World War II** (1939–1945) saw rocket technology progress in leaps and bounds as part of the arms race to make intercontinental missiles.

🪐 **In 1957,** the Soviet Union (USSR, Russia and its allies) launched the first artificial satellite, Sputnik 1, into space.

🪐 **A dog, Laika**, was the first living creature in space on the Soviet Sputnik 2 satellite in 1957.

The 'Space Race'

🪐 **The 1957** launch of the Soviet Sputnik 1 took the world's other superpower, the United States, by surprise.

🪐 **The USA and USSR,** were already locked in a battle of propaganda and superiority in science, technology and armaments, following disagreements after World War II.

🪐 **The USA quickly responded** by launching its own series of satellites. Explorer I was launched in 1958 from Cape Canaveral, Florida, USA.

▼ *The USA's Vanguard 1 was a tiny satellite just 15 cm in diameter. The USSR gave it the nickname of the 'grapefruit' as an insult.*

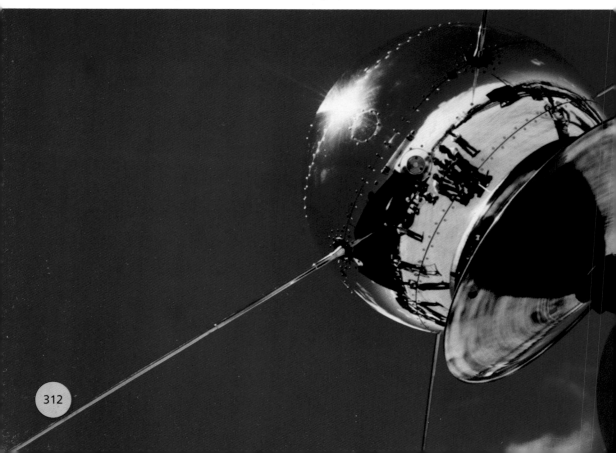

 **A few weeks** later the USA launched Vanguard 1. Meanwhile the USSR continued with its Sputnik launches.

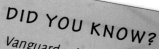
 **Both the USSR and USA** tried to better each other by launching bigger, more complex satellites. Their rivalry became known as the 'Space Race'. It helped space science to progress much faster than if only one nation had been involved.

 **Through the early to late 1960s** the USSR led the race by scoring several notable firsts.

The first manned space flight was made in April 1961 by the Soviet cosmonaut Yuri Gagarin in Vostok 1.

In February 1966, the first controlled Moon landing was made by the Soviet Luna 9.

In 1970, the Soviet Venera 7 was the first probe to touch down on another planet (Venus).

However the USA had turned its attention to another, even bigger first – the first astronauts to land on the Moon.

Modern space travel

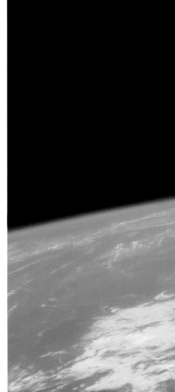

🪐 **During the late 1960s** and early 1970s, US Apollo astronauts became the first to reach another world when six missions travelled to land on the Moon.

🪐 **The arrival of the US space shuttle** – a reusable spaceplane – in 1981 made working in orbit much easier.

🪐 **In the main shuttle cabin** the crew enjoyed comfortable conditions and room to move around.

🪐 **Meanwhile the USSR** was focusing on space stations. In 1986 it set up the first large orbiting station suitable for long-term human occupation, called *Mir*.

🪐 **In 1994–1995** cosmonaut (Russian astronaut) Valeri Poliakov spent 437 days on board the *Mir* space station. This remains the longest continuous stay by a person in space.

🪐 **By the year 2000** unmanned space probes had visited all of the eight planets in the Solar System, but no humans had ventured beyond the Moon.

🪐 **Astronauts have lived** on the International Space Station (ISS) since 2001. Some stay for a few weeks, others for six months or more.

By the mid 2010s more than 550 people had travelled into space. An average of 10–12 now go each year. However if space tourism takes off this number may well increase three to five times.

▼ *An unmanned SpaceX Dragon supply craft is captured by the robotic arm on the International Space Station, in preparation for docking (full attachment).*

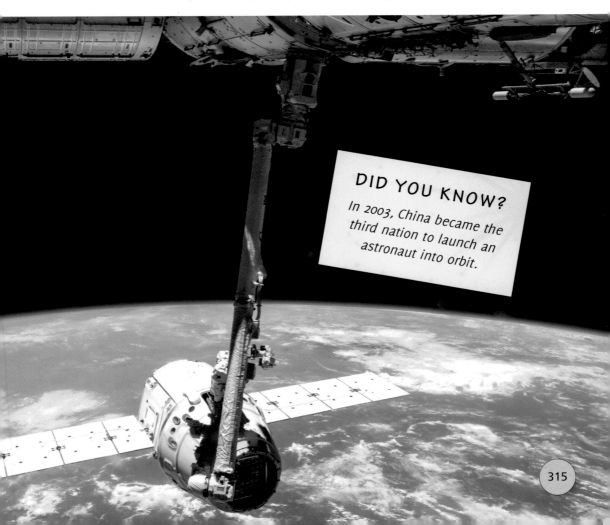

DID YOU KNOW?

In 2003, China became the third nation to launch an astronaut into orbit.

Space exploration

Space is explored in two ways – by studying it from Earth using powerful telescopes, and by launching spacecraft to get a closer view.

Most space exploration is by unmanned spacecraft, usually called robotic craft or probes.

The first pictures of the far side of the Moon were sent back by the *Luna 3* space probe in October 1959.

Manned missions have only reached as far as the Moon and no one has been back there since 1972.

Apollo astronauts took three days to reach the Moon.

Apart from Apollo, a space probe has never come back to Earth's surface from a moon, planet or other space body.

However sample return missions have brought back rocks, dust and other material, such as rocks from the Moon by Apollo, comet material in 2006 by the *Stardust* probe, and asteroid samples in 2010 by Japan's *Hayabusa* craft.

DID YOU KNOW?
NASA hopes to send astronauts back to the Moon by 2030, perhaps followed by manned missions to Mars.

▲ *The first successful planetary probe was the USA's Mariner 2,*
which flew past Venus in 1962.

Spacecraft

- **There are three kinds of spacecraft** – artificial orbiting satellites, unmanned probes and manned spacecraft.

- **Almost all spacecraft have double hulls** (outer coverings) for protection against other space objects that may crash into them.

- **Manned spacecraft must also contain** air under pressure to prevent the crew's blood from boiling.

- **Manned spacecraft have life-support systems** that provide oxygen to breathe, usually mixed with nitrogen (as in ordinary air).

- **The carbon dioxide that the crew** breathes out is absorbed by chemicals such as zeolite or lithium hydroxide. The air is refreshed with oxygen made by splitting water (H_2O) using electricity.

- **Spacecraft windows have filters** to shield astronauts from the Sun's dangerous ultraviolet rays.

- **Radiators on the outside** of the spacecraft remove excess heat from electrical equipment and the crew's bodies.

- **Astronauts use a waterproof shower** that sprays water from all sides and then removes the waste water.

- **Spacecraft toilets** need to get rid of waste in low gravity conditions. Astronauts have to sit on a device that sucks away the waste. Solid waste is dried and returned to Earth.

> **DID YOU KNOW?**
> Astronauts would float when asleep if they were not strapped down in a sleeping bag.

▲ Between 1981 and 2011 the US space shuttles, the first and only reusable spacecraft so far, made 135 manned space flights into orbit and back to Earth.

Astronauts

🪐 **The first astronauts** were jet pilots.

🪐 **In the USA** anyone who has flown at an altitude of more than 80 km above sea level, which includes some aircraft test pilots, is awarded 'astronaut wings'.

🪐 **The US space shuttle carried** three kinds of astronaut – pilots, mission specialists and payload specialists.

🪐 **A pilot or commander's job** is to be responsible for the mission and to control the spacecraft.

🪐 **Mission specialists** are crew members who carry out specific jobs, such as running experiments or going on space walks.

🪐 **Payload specialists** are not NASA astronauts, but scientists and other onboard guests.

🪐 **Astronauts on long missions** use exercise machines to keep fit and avoid problems such as muscle wasting.

🪐 **The first woman in space** was Soviet cosmonaut Valentina Tereshkova, who completed 48 orbits of the Earth in June 1963.

🪐 **The first space tourist** was American Dennis Tito. He is reported to have paid $20 million to spend nearly eight days aboard a Russian *Soyuz* spacecraft in 2001. Several other people have subsequently paid their own ticket to get into space.

DID YOU KNOW?
Weightlessness makes astronauts become a few centimetres taller during a long mission.

▼ *Astronauts train for years. They learn to fly in simulators and in training aircraft before dealing with the demands of space missions.*

Take-off

▼ *The US space shuttle used two boosters to help it overcome Earth's gravity and rise into orbit.*

3 Main fuel tank falls away 130 km up – this is the second stage

2 Solid-fuel rocket burners fall away 45 km up – this is the first stage

1 Shuttle blasts off using its engines and two solid rocket boosters

When a spacecraft is launched, it needs to overcome the pull of Earth's gravity by being launched at a particular velocity (speed and direction).

The minimum velocity needed for a spacecraft to combat gravity and stay in orbit around Earth is called the orbital velocity.

When a spacecraft at launch reaches 140 percent of the orbital velocity, it can break free of Earth's gravity. This is called the escape velocity.

Earth's escape velocity is approximately 11.2 km/sec, or 40,300 km/h.

The thrust (push) that launches a spacecraft comes from powerful rocket engines in launch vehicles.

▶ *Russia's Soyuz vehicles have been the mainstay of their space programme since the 1960s. This Soyuz FG rocket took a Soyuz TMA-M spacecraft with Yuri Malenchenko, Tim Kopra and Tim Peake to the ISS in 2015.*

- **Some launch vehicles** are divided into stages, one on top of another, which fall away as their task is done.

- **The first stage lifts** everything off the ground, so its thrust must be greater than the weight of the launch vehicle plus the spacecraft. It falls away a few minutes after take off.

- **A second stage is then needed** to accelerate the spacecraft towards space.

- **After the two launch stages fall away,** there may be a third stage to put or insert the spacecraft into orbit.

- **An alternative design** is to use booster rockets which also fall away, or jettison, from the main vehicle when they finish firing.

- **To stay in Low Earth Orbit,** say 200 km above Earth, a spacecraft must fly at more than 8 km/sec.

323

Early rockets

🪐 **The only machines** that can provide the huge thrust needed to overcome the pull of Earth's gravity and launch a spacecraft into space are rocket engines or rocket motors.

🪐 **The first rockets** were made 1000 years ago in China, powered by gunpowder. But they lacked the ability to go to heights of more than about one kilometre.

🪐 **The first liquid-propelled rockets** suitable for space travel date from the 1920s from the USA, Russia and Germany.

🪐 **During World War II** German rocket designer Werner von Braun (1912–1977) and his teams developed several kinds of rockets as long-distance weapons, especially the Vergeltungswaffen 2 (Revenge Weapon 2), usually called the V2.

🪐 **In 1944** a V2 on a test flight was the first man-made object to go into space above a height of 100 km. It reached an estimated altitude of 180 km.

🪐 **After World War II** V2s were developed further in the USA by von Braun and led to much bigger rockets.

🪐 **In 1948 the Bumper series** of US rockets flew higher and higher, eventually reaching almost 400 km.

🪐 **Meanwhile the USSR** was developing its own rockets, including the space-capable R–7 Semyorka. It first flew in 1957 and a later version launched Sputnik 1 the same year.

DID YOU KNOW?
The most powerful rocket ever was Saturn 5, which sent US astronauts to the Moon.

▼ *Robert Goddard launched the first liquid-fuel rocket in 1926. 'Nell' stayed in the air for 2.5 seconds and climbed to a height of 12 m.*

How rockets work

🪐 **A space launch vehicle is sometimes** called a rocket, but the rocket engine is only one part of this huge and powerful machine.

🪐 **Hot gases that drive a rocket engine** and its launch vehicle upwards are produced when the engine burns propellant.

▼ *A US J-2X rocket engine is tested to check its gimbals – swivels or pivots that tilt the nozzle outlet to alter the direction of the thrust and keep the rocket on course.*

🪐 **Rocket propellants come in two parts** – a fuel and an oxidizer.

🪐 **The fuel is a chemical that burns** or combusts to produce vast amounts of hot gases. These blast out of the engine to provide the pushing force or thrust.

🪐 **The oxidizer is a chemical** that is necessary for the fuel to burn. Combustion is a chemical reaction which needs oxygen. There is no oxygen (or much else) in space, so rocket engines need to take their own supplies.

🪐 **In a solid fuel rocket**, the fuel and oxidizer are chemicals mixed together to make a rubbery substance. Once lit or ignited, it usually burns until it runs out, with little control.

🪐 **Whereas in a liquid fuel rocket**, the fuel and oxidizer are in liquid form and their flow can be controlled by tap-like valves.

🪐 **Liquid fuel** is sometimes liquid hydrogen, and it is typically used in big rockets. Another form is kerosene or paraffin (as used in homes, lamps and stoves).

🪐 **The oxidizer** may be liquid oxygen, called 'LOx' for short. Other substances that contain a large amount of oxygen include nitrogen tetroxide and hydrogen peroxide.

Other propulsion

🪐 **Rocket motors** are useful for launching or propelling vehicles into space, but they are impractical for long distance travel because of the weight of fuel and oxidizer needed to power the motor.

🪐 **Alternative means** of propulsion for space vehicles include the ion drive engine.

🪐 **Ion drive engines** use an electrical field to ionize atoms and accelerate them out of the back of the engine. This stream of ions produces the thrust that drives the spacecraft forwards.

🪐 **An additional advantage of the ion drive** engine is that it can run at full throttle for months without deteriorating.

🪐 **For journeys within the Solar System**, some scientists plan to use spacecraft that will be propelled by harnessing the power of the Sun with a solar sail.

🪐 **The proposed solar sail** would be at least 1000 m across and made of a highly reflective material. The force of sunlight and the solar wind against the sail would push the craft gently away from the Sun.

🪐 **A more controversial idea** is to use nuclear engines to power spacecraft. Some experiments were carried out in the 1960s but were discontinued because of public fears about radiation.

🪐 **In its crudest form**, a nuclear space engine consists of a series of small atomic bombs exploded against the underside of an immensely strong, dish-shaped metal structure.

🪐 **More futuristic ideas for interstellar travel** include the hydrogen ram-scoop engine that would collect fuel from clouds of interstellar gas as it went along, fission-fragment engines that break apart atoms, and antimatter engines.

🪐 **The Dawn space probe** launched in 2007 is powered by three xenon ion thrusters.

▼ *Dawn was the first probe to use solely ion thrusters for propulsion. It has three, with one in use at a time. They are fuelled by 425 kg of the rare gas xenon in liquid form. The craft travelled to the Main Asteroid Belt to visit Vesta, and now orbits dwarf planet Ceres.*

Satellites

🪐 **Objects that orbit planets** and other space objects are called satellites.

🪐 **Moons are natural satellites** of planets, while planets are natural satellites of their star, such as Earth around the Sun.

🪐 **Spacecraft that orbit Earth**, or the Moon, or another planet or moon, or even an asteroid or a comet, are known as artificial satellites.

🪐 **The first artificial satellite** was Sputnik 1, launched on 4 October 1957.

🪐 **Over 50 artificial satellites** are now launched every year. A few of them are space telescopes or observatories.

🪐 **Navigation satellites** (navsats), such as the 32 satellites involved in the Global Positioning System (GPS), are used by people in ships, planes and vehicles to work out where they are.

🪐 **Communications satellites** (comsats) relay – receive and send on – communications as radio waves or microwaves, including phone calls, computer data, TV and radio, and internet traffic.

🪐 **Weather (meteorological) satellites** (meteosats) measure clouds, rain, snow, temperature, air pressure, waves and other aspects of weather and climate.

🪐 **Survey satellites** measure and photograph Earth's surface in great detail, monitoring events such as earthquakes and tsunamis.

🪐 **Spy satellites** watch developments such as missile movements and listen into all kinds of communications.

▼ *The USA launched five THEMIS satellites in 2007 to study the Earth's magnetic field. Each weighed about 78 kg and all five were packed into the top of a Delta II launcher, inside the streamlined nose cone or fairing.*

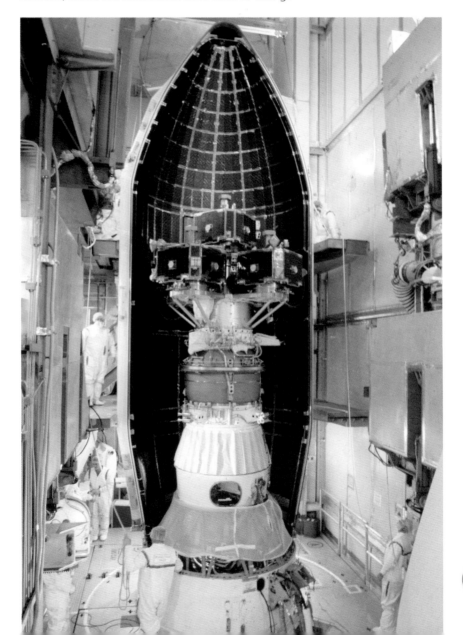

How orbits work

🪐 **An orbit is the path** of one space object around a larger one, held by the pull of gravity. Moons orbit planets and planets orbit stars.

🪐 **Orbits may be circular**, elliptical (oval) or parabolic (open). The orbits of the planets around the Sun are elliptical.

🪐 **An orbiting space object** is called a satellite.

🪐 **Stars in the Milky Way galaxy**, such as the Sun, have the longest known orbits. They can take up to 250 million years to orbit the galaxy's centre.

🪐 **The force of momentum** keeps a satellite moving through space. The amount of momentum a satellite has depends on its mass and on its velocity (speed and direction).

🪐 **A satellite orbits** at the height where its momentum exactly balances the pull of gravity.

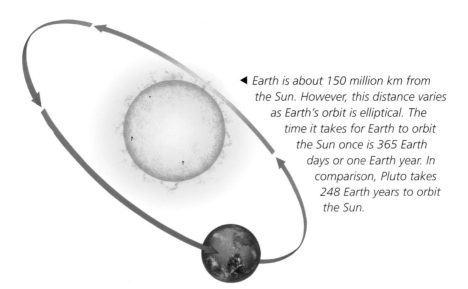

◀ Earth is about 150 million km from the Sun. However, this distance varies as Earth's orbit is elliptical. The time it takes for Earth to orbit the Sun once is 365 Earth days or one Earth year. In comparison, Pluto takes 248 Earth years to orbit the Sun.

If the gravitational pull is greater than a satellite's momentum, the satellite falls in towards the object it is orbiting.

If a satellite's momentum is greater than the pull of gravity, it flies off and away into space.

The lower a satellite orbits, the faster it must travel to stop it falling in towards the larger space object.

Conversely, the higher a satellite orbits, the slower it can travel.

A satellite in an elliptical orbit slows down at the farthest distance and speeds up as it gets nearer.

◀ The planets in the Solar System all move round the Sun in elliptical orbits.

Types of orbits

🪐 **There are various kinds** of Earth orbits for satellites and other spacecraft.

🪐 **Low Earth Orbit** (LEO) is one of the most common, especially for craft that have just launched.

▼ *Higher orbits are slower. A low LEO, less than 200 km high, involves speeds of more than 28,000 km/h and an orbital time of less than 90 minutes. GEO satellites 35,785 km high travel at 11,160 km/h for an orbital time of 23 hours 56 minutes.*

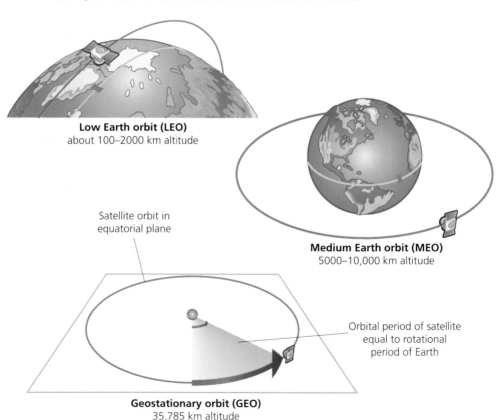

Low Earth orbit (LEO)
about 100–2000 km altitude

Satellite orbit in
equatorial plane

Medium Earth orbit (MEO)
5000–10,000 km altitude

Orbital period of satellite
equal to rotational
period of Earth

Geostationary orbit (GEO)
35,785 km altitude

- **LEOs** vary from 150 km to 1900 km high (above sea level), and orbital times of 86 to 125 minutes.

- **In geostationary orbit (GEO)** a satellite or other craft orbits Earth above the Equator once in the same time the planet takes to rotate once.

DID YOU KNOW?

All human spacecraft and space stations have involved LEOs, apart from suborbital 'hops' up and straight down again.

- **A GEO satellite** seems to hang above the same place on Earth's surface, meaning dishes or other antennae (aerials) do not have to move to follow it.

- **A GEO satellite** must be 35,785 km high.

- **GEOs are used** by many communications satellites such as those that broadcast satellite television signals.

- **A Sun-synchronous orbit** alters its angle and position around Earth so that, when seen from the Sun, a satellite or other craft always looks at the same angle – and its solar panels receive a lot of sunlight.

Space probes

🪐 **Space can be explored using probes** – unmanned, automatic, robotic, computer-controlled spacecraft.

🪐 **Some probes simply make a flyby** or close approach of a space object. Others, called orbiters, go into orbit around it. Some, known as landers, make a soft touchdown on the surface. A few, called rovers, are able to move around on the surface.

▼ *Japan's Hayabusa probe, launched in 2003, had several setbacks on its immense mission. But it also scored several 'firsts', including bringing samples of asteroid Itokawa back to Earth in 2010.*

- **The first successful planetary probe** was the USA's Mariner 2, which flew past Venus in 1962.

- **In 1974**, Mariner 10 made a flyby of Mercury.

- **Viking 1 and 2 landed** on Mars in 1976.

- **Voyager 2 has flown** 10 billion km and is heading out of the Solar System after passing close to Jupiter (1979), Saturn (1981), Uranus (1986) and Neptune (1989).

- **To save fuel on journeys** to distant planets, space probes may use a nearby planet's gravity to catapult them on their way. This is called a slingshot.

- **Various orbiters** have visited Venus and Mars, mapping their surfaces in great detail.

- **Landers have reached the Moon**, Venus, Mars, Saturn's moon Titan, asteroids Eros and Itokawa, and comet Churyumov–Gerasimenko.

- **Rovers have explored** the surface of the Moon and Mars.

- **The New Horizons probe** was launched in 2006 and reached Pluto in 2015.

Pioneers 10 and 11

Pioneers 10 and 11 are two US space probes that were launched in the 1970s to study the Main Belt asteroids and outer planets.

Both craft were very similar, with a mass at launch of 270 kg and a dishlike antenna 2.7 m across.

Pioneer 10 took off in 1972 as one of the fastest craft to leave Earth, at 52,000 km/h.

Later that year it crossed the Main Belt. Then in 1973, travelling at 132,000 km/h, it flew past Jupiter at less than 130,000 km distance.

Pioneer 10 took the first close-up images of Jupiter, studied its radiation and magnetic field, and discovered its liquid interior. It then headed out of the Solar System.

Pioneer 11 left Earth in 1973, passed through the Main Belt in 1974, and later that year flew within 43,000 km of Jupiter. Here it studied the Great Red Spot and Jupiter's polar regions, and its moon Callisto.

Next flyby was Saturn in 1979, approaching to within 20,000 km to take the first close-ups, discover new moons and find a new ring.

Both Pioneers are still heading away from the Solar System, and will continue to do so unless they collide with a piece of space rock (a very remote chance).

Last contact with Pioneer 10 was in 2002 and with Pioneer 11 in 1995.

▲ *The Pioneers are now at the edge of the Solar System, with Pioneer 11 more than 90 AUs distant (90 times farther than Earth from the Sun). Pioneer 10 is over 110 AUs away and may reach the vicinity of the star Aldebran in about two million years.*

339

Voyagers 1 and 2

🪐 **The Voyagers are a pair** of unmanned US space probes, launched to explore the outer planets. They are still in space.

🪐 **Voyager 1 was launched** on 5 September 1977. It flew past Jupiter in March 1979 and Saturn in November 1980, then continued on a curved path to take it out of the Solar System altogether.

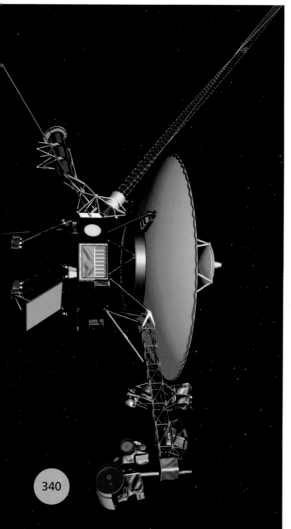

🪐 **Voyager 2 travelled** more slowly. Although it was launched two weeks earlier than Voyager 1, it did not reach Jupiter until July 1979 and Saturn until August 1981.

🪐 **Both Voyagers used** the slingshot effect of Jupiter's gravity to hurl them on towards Saturn.

🪐 **While Voyager 1 headed out** of the Solar System, Voyager 2 flew on and passed Uranus in January 1986.

🪐 **Voyager 2 then passed** Neptune on 25 August 1989. It took close-up photographs of Uranus and Neptune.

◀ *Voyager 1 flew close to Jupiter and Saturn. Its radio dish for sending and receiving information is 3.7 m across. It is now the most distant man-made object from Earth.*

🪐 **The Voyagers revealed** volcanoes on Io, one of Jupiter's Galilean moons.

🪐 **Voyager 2 found ten moons** around Uranus.

🪐 **Six moons and five rings** around Neptune were also discovered by Voyager 2.

DID YOU KNOW?
Voyager 1 and 2 will beam back data perhaps past 2020 as they travel out of the Solar System.

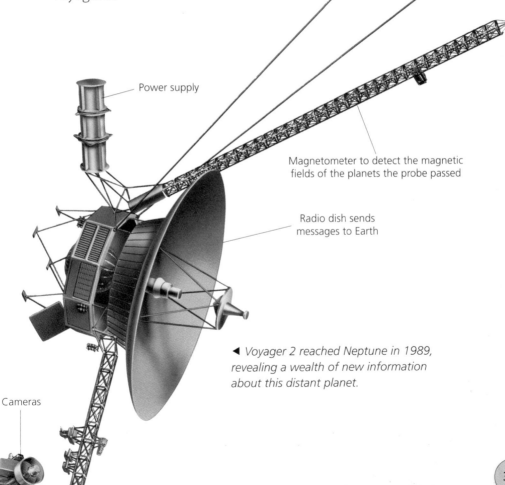

Power supply

Magnetometer to detect the magnetic fields of the planets the probe passed

Radio dish sends messages to Earth

Cameras

◄ *Voyager 2 reached Neptune in 1989, revealing a wealth of new information about this distant planet.*

341

Space stations

- **A space station** is a man-made structure in space designed for humans (or perhaps animals) to survive for at least days, usually months, even years.

- **Most space stations are designed** to orbit a planet. The only ones built and inhabited so far orbit Earth.

🪐 **There is neither an up nor a down** in a space station, since objects and people are weightless due to the lack of gravity.

🪐 **The first Earth space station** was the Soviet *Salyut 1*, launched in April 1971.

🪐 *Salyut 1* **was occupied** for 24 days by the crew of Soviet spacecraft *Soyuz 11*. Sadly they perished as their spacecraft re-entered Earth's atmosphere.

🪐 *Salyut 1* **had a very low orbit** and limited fuel. After the crew disaster, it was de-orbited and itself broke up during re-entry.

🪐 *Skylab* **was the first US space station**. Three crews spent a total of 171 days there in 1973–1974.

🪐 **Launched in 1986,** the Soviet station *Mir* made more than 89,000 orbits of Earth. The last crew left in 2000.

🪐 **The giant International Space Station (ISS)** was built in stages starting in 1998. The first crew boarded in November 2000.

◀ *The Columbus module of the ISS is 6.9 m long and was attached in 2008. It was built by the ESA and contains mainly science equipment for experiments and recordings, from the effects of spaceflight on the human body to an incredibly accurate atomic clock that measures if time passes more slowly on board.*

343

Skylab

- **The first US space station**, *Skylab* was launched in 1973 into Low Earth Orbit, 440 km above Earth.

- *Skylab* had workshops, living quarters, research equipment and an observatory called ATM with four telescopes and other devices.

- *Skylab* **was based** on the Saturn rocket launch vehicle. It was constructed from a Saturn 1B second stage and was 26.3 m long, 17 m wide with its solar panel, 7.4 m tall, and had a mass of 77 tonnes.

- **The station was launched** (without crew) by a giant Saturn V rocket – as used for Apollo moonshots. *Skylab* was Saturn V's last lift-off.

- **The station received** three sets of three crew between 1973 and 1974, each brought up by an adapted Apollo craft on a Saturn 1B launcher.

- **During launch** the station's heat and meteoroid shield tore off, removing one solar panel as well, and jamming the other. This meant *Skylab* had very little electrical power.

- **The first crew spacewalked** to fix a replacement heat shield and free the solar panel.

- *Skylab*'s **crews** made a total of 10 spacewalks and carried out hundreds of experiments in microgravity.

▶ Skylab, *America's first experimental space station launched in 1973 and soon hosted its first crew, which conducted solar astronomy and earth resources experiments, medical studies, and five student experiments. Two other crews followed later that year.*

Skylab **carried out** new studies of the Sun, looking especially at solar flares and coronal holes.

After 2249 days of 15.4 orbits per day, *Skylab*'s altitude faded. It burned up on re-entry into Earth's atmosphere – mostly, with some bits landing in Western Australia.

Mir

🪐 **The Soviet/Russian space station** *Mir*, meaning peace, began operation in 1986.

🪐 *Mir* **was assembled** from one core module, or central section, and six additional modules, all carried by separate launchers.

🪐 **The fifth of these**, the docking module, was brought up by a US space shuttle in 1995. The final addition was Priroda, the Earth Sensing Module, to image and study Earth and its resources.

🪐 **When finally assembled**, *Mir* measured 31 m by 19 m by 27.5 m, with a mass of 130 tonnes.

🪐 *Mir's* **orbit averaged** a height of 360 km, taking 92 minutes per orbit at an average speed of 27,700 km/h.

🪐 *Mir's* **standard crew** was three, and over its life the station was home to 104 astronauts from 12 nations, who carried out 80 spacewalks.

🪐 **Russian Valeri Polyakov** holds the record for the longest single trip in space, staying on *Mir* for 437 days 18 hours in 1994–1995.

🪐 **The** *Shuttle-Mir* **programme** saw the US and Russia cooperating in space.

🪐 **In February 1995**, shuttle *Discovery* flew near to *Mir* to practise joining or docking. In June that year, shuttle *Atlantis* docked with *Mir* to bring new crew members and take away others.

🪐 *Mir* **gradually fell into disrepair** with many small faults. After the final crew visit in 2000, it was decided to deorbit the station. In 2001 it burned up on re-entry over the South Pacific.

▲ Russia's Mir *space station, connected to* Atlantis *space shuttle. Mir made 76,000 orbits of Earth before it was crashed into the Pacific Ocean in 2001.*

International Space Station (ISS)

🪐 **The ISS**, International Space Station, is a multi-nation Earth-orbiting station.

🪐 **Russian launchers** and US space shuttles were involved in its construction, but since the shuttles retired in 2011, most missions for cargo and crew use Russian Soyuz launchers and craft.

🪐 **The first section of module**, Zarya (meaning 'dawn'), was sent up in 1998. It is now mainly used for storage.

🪐 **When the most recent** (14th) main module, Leonardo, was added in 2011, the ISS was 73 m long, 108 m wide and 20 m high, with a mass of 450 tonnes.

🪐 **Three or four further modules** may be added to the ISS by 2022.

🪐 **The ISS orbits** at an average altitude of 410 km and can be seen with the unaided eye from Earth as sunlight reflects off it.

🪐 **The orbital height** slowly reduces, so the ISS is regularly boosted back to correct height by visiting spacecraft.

🪐 **Its orbital speed** is 27,600 km/h and each orbit lasts nearly 93 minutes.

🪐 **The smallest crews** on the ISS numbered two, the usual is six, and the maximum is seven.

🪐 **Several space tourists** have paid to travel to the ISS. First was US engineer Dennis Tito.

▼ *The ISS is made of separate modules fitted together in space. It is powered by huge solar panels. This photo shows a US space shuttle docked on one of the last shuttle missions.*

Space suits

- **Astronauts wear space suits** for protection when they go outside their spacecraft. The suits are also called EMUs (Extra-vehicular Mobility Units).

- **The outer layers of a space suit** protect against harmful radiation from the Sun and fast-moving particles of space dust called micrometeoroids.

- **The clear, plastic-composite helmet** also protects against radiation and micrometeoroids.

- **Oxygen is circulated** around the helmet to prevent the visor from misting.

- **The middle layers of a space suit** are blown up like a balloon to press against the astronaut's body. Without this pressure, the astronaut's blood would boil.

- **Space suits have a soft inner lining** that contains tubes of water to cool the astronaut's body.

- **The backpack supplies pure oxygen** for the astronaut to breathe, and gets rid of the carbon dioxide that is breathed out. The oxygen tank can supply the astronaut for up to eight hours.

- **There are various glove designs**. Some have silicone-rubber fingertips, which allow the astronaut some sense of touch.

- **Various parts in the suit** deal with liquids, including a tube for drinks and another for urine.

- **The full cost of the latest space suit** is more than $10 million (£6.5 million), although about half of this is for the backpack and control module.

▲ Crew member and flight engineer Sergey Ryazansky wears the latest version of the Russian Orlan space suit, an Orlan MK. The original Orlan suits date back to 1977.

Space walks

🪐 **The technical name** for going outside a spacecraft is Extra-Vehicular Activity (EVA).

🪐 **In 1965, Soviet cosmonaut Alexei Leonov** was the first person to walk in space.

🪐 **During space walks** a cable (called an umbilical) in some space suits keeps the astronauts connected to their spacecraft.

🪐 **A Manned Manoeuvring Unit (MMU)** was a rocket-powered backpack that allowed astronauts to go further from their spacecraft.

🪐 **In 1984, US astronaut Bruce McCandless** was the first person to use an MMU in space.

🪐 **Damages and alterations to various spacecraft**, including the *Skylab* and *Mir* space stations, the Hubble Space Telescope, and various satellites, have been repaired by space-walking astronauts.

🪐 **The longest space walks** were 8 hours 56 minutes by US astronauts Susan Helms and Jim Voss in March 2001. They carried out preparations for a new unit to join, or dock with, the ISS.

🪐 **Russian and US astronauts** use robotic arms to help them modify sections of the ISS.

DID YOU KNOW?
Astronauts on space walks may be aided by a flying robot camera the size of a beach ball.

▶ *US astronauts cooperate during a space shuttle mission. The red leg bands identify which astronaut is which.*

Working in space

- **On board the ISS**, astronauts have varied work tasks. Many are specialists in using a particular piece of equipment or experiment.

- **Science areas** include human and animal biology, medicine, astronomy and other space sciences, meteorology (Earth weather), engineering, atmospherics, materials and chemicals.

- **Some of the experiments** look at how conditions with almost no gravity affects chemicals, materials and living things.

- **There are regular astronaut spacewalks** outside the ISS to check for problems, install new equipment and make adjustments.

- **The main robotic arm** is Canadarm2, with a length of 17.6 m and joints worked by electric motors. It has a mass of 1.8 tonnes but so far above Earth it is almost weightless.

🪐 **Canadarm2** helps spacewalking astronauts and can move itself around the ISS using an inchworm caterpillar-like action.

🪐 **In 2011** a new worker arrived at the ISS – Dextre. Also called the Special Purpose Dexterous Manipulator (SPDM), it is a robot with two arms 3.5 m long.

🪐 **Dextre is moved by Canadarm2** and has viewing cameras and a wide range of tools for many different tasks.

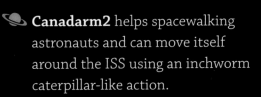

DID YOU KNOW?
Many animals have been to the ISS, including butterflies, crickets, fish, frogs, fruit-flies, mice, quails, snails and spiders.

◄ *Dextre is the ISS 'handyman'. It has heaters to keep its motors and electronics warm and working well.*

355

Apollo to the Moon

🪐 **In 1961 US President John F Kennedy** declared: 'I believe that this nation should commit itself to achieving the goal, before this decade is out, of landing a man on the moon and returning him safely to the Earth.'

🪐 **The three-man Apollo set-up** included the CSM (Command/ Service Modules). Astronauts lived in the cone-shaped Command Module, with most equipment in the cylindrical Service Module.

🪐 **The Lunar Module** (LM) was the Moon lander, with a descent stage base for landing on the Moon, and an ascent stage to take off.

🪐 **After unmanned test flights**, *Apollo 7* took off in October 1968 to orbit Earth.

🪐 **In November** *Apollo 8* went to the Moon and orbited 10 times before returning.

🪐 **In March 1969** *Apollo 9* tested various docking and other manoeuvres and spacesuits while in Earth orbit.

🪐 **May 1969** saw *Apollo 10*'s test approach within 15 km of the Moon's surface.

🪐 **In July 1969** *Apollo 11* landed the first astronauts on the Moon.

🪐 **All following missions**, to the final *Apollo 17* in December 1972, landed on the Moon – except one.

🪐 **After two days**, *Apollo 13* suffered a liquid oxygen tank explosion. The astronauts looped around the Moon and returned safely to Earth.

DID YOU KNOW?
Stricken Apollo 13's motto was 'Ex Luna, Scientia', meaning 'From the Moon, knowledge'.

▲ *The last Apollo mission, Apollo 17, returned to Earth in December 1972. The descending capsules were watched by aircraft and helicopters and splashed down in the Pacific Ocean.*

One small step…

▼ *In 1971, James Irwin stands beside his landing craft with his Moon car, called a Lunar Rover.*

- *Apollo 11* launched from the Kennedy Space Center in Florida, USA on 16 July 1969.

- **The three astronauts** were Neil Armstrong, Edwin 'Buzz' Aldrin and Michael Collins.

- **After a three-day trip**, *Apollo 11* reached the Moon and went into lunar orbit.

- **Collins stayed in orbit** in the CSM, Command/Service Modules, called Columbia.

- **Armstrong and Aldrin** transferred to the LM, Lunar Module, called Eagle, and disconnected from the CSM.

- **The LM descended** and landed in the Sea of Tranquillity, a site on the Moon's surface chosen for its flat landscape.

- **However the area had many boulders**. Armstrong had to take the controls and find a flatter place, which he did with less than 30 seconds of fuel left.

- **At 2.56 am (UTC) on 20 July 1969**, Armstrong stepped onto the surface and declared: 'That's one small step for man, one giant leap for mankind.'

- **Aldrin also left the LM** for a moon walk as the two recorded their experiences and collected moon rocks and dust.

- **After about 21 hours on the surface**, the two astronauts took off in the LM ascent stage, rejoined Collins in the CSM, and returned to Earth. They splashed down in the CM into the Pacific Ocean on 24 July.

21st-century Moon exploration

🪐 **The Moon** has been visited by dozens of spacecraft since 1959.

🪐 **Missions since 2000** include India's Chandrayaan-1 and the US LRO/LCROSS (see Moon probes).

🪐 **China's exploration** began with the Chang'e 1 probe, named after China's traditional Moon goddess, in 2007. It orbited the Moon for 17 months, and captured many detailed pictures.

🪐 **In 2010 Chang'e 2** made even more comprehensive Moon maps, then flew past asteroid Toutatis in 2012.

🪐 **Chang'e 3** left Earth in 2013 and landed on the Moon. It was the first soft-landing on the surface since 1976.

🪐 **This mission carried** a small rover named Yutu, meaning 'jade rabbit'. It is about 1.5 m long with a mass of 135 kg.

🪐 **About one month** after starting its exploration, Yutu suffered a failure and could not move. It continued to send information until late 2014.

🪐 **In 2013** the US sent the Lunar Atmosphere and Dust Environment Explorer (LADEE) to the Moon. It was deliberately impacted on the far side in 2014, at a speed of almost 6000 km/h, watched by the Lunar Reconnaissance Orbiter.

🪐 **Planned Moon missions** include China's Chang'e 4 to return samples to Earth, India's Chandrayaan 2 with two rovers, and Russia's Luna-Glob 1 to scout for a possible Moon base site.

▲ China's Yutu rover worked well at first. But part of its control circuits failed and it could not fold its solar panels over itself as a 'blanket' against the extremely cold lunar night, so gradually the rest of its equipment deteriorated.

Rovers on Mars

▼ On its short mast (upper left), Curiosity has twin colour television cameras for a 3D view. Above them in the white box is a laser to fire at soil and rocks – the light given off by the target is observed and analyzed for various chemicals.

🪐 **Four rovers have roamed across** the surface of Mars, all of them sent by the US. They include the twin Mars Exploration Rovers (MERs) Opportunity and Spirit, as well as Curiosity, which is part of the Mars Science Laboratory (MSL) mission.

🪐 **MER-B Opportunity and MER-A Spirit** left Earth three weeks apart in 2003 and landed on Mars one year later on opposite sides of the planet.

🪐 **Each rover is 1.5 m high** and 1.6 m long. Each mission was designed to last about 90 solar days, but both far outperformed this time.

🪐 **Spirit was active until 2009**, travelling more than 7.7 km, until it became stuck in soft soil. However it continued to send information for another year before contact was finally lost.

🪐 **Opportunity continued to travel** and has been sending back information for more than 50 times its original mission time.

🪐 **The much larger**, almost car-sized Curiosity was launched in November 2011 and landed in August 2012 in Mars' Gale Crater. It has a dozen scientific instruments and detectors, and a 2.1-m robot arm with five tools and devices at the end.

🪐 **Curiosity's drill** can make holes up to 5 cm deep. The resulting rock particles are then scooped up and analyzed.

🪐 **Curiosity can trundle over rocks** and other objects up to 60 cm high, using its six wheels. Each wheel, 50 cm across, has its own suspension arm and electric motor.

🪐 **There are eight hazcams**, or hazard cameras, four at the front and four at the rear. They see a wide view and look for boulders, ridges and other problems that Curiosity then steers around.

Mission to Mars?

▼ *An artist's impression of a future Mars landing. With their spacecraft in orbit, astronauts would descend to the planet's surface in an excursion vehicle. This would later carry them back into orbit to rendezvous with their spacecraft.*

DID YOU KNOW?

The earliest date of a manned Mars mission is very unlikely to be before 2040.

🪐 **A manned mission to Mars** is possible with existing technology, but it would be extremely expensive. Current estimates of the cost vary from $5 billion (£3.2 billion) to 100 times that amount.

🪐 **Astronauts who visit Mars** would face many hazards. They would be exposed to high-energy cosmic rays during the 200-day journey and they would have to avoid the Martian dust-storm season, which lasts 14 Earth months.

🪐 **Radio messages** can take as long as 18 minutes to travel between Earth and Mars, so the Martian astronauts would experience considerable communications lag if they needed the assistance of Earth-based mission controllers during an emergency.

🪐 **One suggestion for a Mars mission** is to use a new single large launch vehicle to put a completed Mars spacecraft into orbit around the Earth.

🪐 **An alternative suggestion** is to load the components of the Mars spacecraft aboard a number of smaller and cheaper launch vehicles, and then assemble them in orbit.

🪐 **One joint American-European mission** proposed two spacecraft – one to carry six astronauts and the other to carry their supplies and equipment. The mission would take an estimated 450 days, with three astronauts spending 60 days on the surface of Mars.

🪐 **Some people have volunteered** for a much less expensive option: a one-way mission. They would stay on Mars for life and take part in scientific studies on the planet, astronomy, human health – and in reality television programmes.

Long-distance space travel

🪐 **A return trip to Mars** would take well over one year. What are the prospects for humans travelling farther, to outer planets or even beyond the Solar System?

🪐 **Current spacecraft speeds** are far too slow to be practical. Future ideas involve manipulating the four dimensions of space-time to find 'short-cuts' across vast distances.

One theoretical possibility is the wormhole. A wormhole 'tunnel' might link two very different locations in the Universe and could take as little as a few seconds to pass through.

Rather than a craft passing through space, space could pass by the craft by bending or warping it. This theory is behind faster-than-light warp drive put forward in the American entertainment franchise *Star Trek* and similar science fiction.

Why travel such vast distances at colossal costs? In part because of the natural human desire to explore, discover and increase understanding.

New materials and substances found in faraway worlds could revolutionize life on Earth – and also make a grand commercial profit. Examples include mining asteroids for precious minerals or the possibility of collecting solar energy deep in space.

Another commonly cited reason is that future Earth may suffer so much from global warming, pollution, lack of resources and too many people, that it is not longer habitable. Humanity will have to strike out and find new worlds to survive.

◄ Star Trek: The Next Generation*'s famous fictional starship* USS Enterprise NCC 1701 *is the first main vehicle of that name in the long-running television and movie series. Launched in 2245, this craft has 'warp drive' a technology that allows it to travel many times faster than light. At 289 m the craft is more than four times longer than a Boeing 747 jumbo jet, and carries a basic crew of about 430 humans, Vulcans and others.*

Index

Index

Entries in **bold** refer to main entries; entries in *italics* refer to illustrations.